The Way

40 DAYS OF REFLECTION

D0188282

The Way
Walking in the Footsteps of Jesus

Book
The Way
978-1-4267-5251-3

Devotional
The Way: 40 Days of Reflection
978-1-4267-5252-0

DVD
The Way: DVD with Leader Guide
843504033033

Youth Study
The Way: Youth Study Edition
978-1-4267-5254-4

Children's Study
The Way: Children's Leader Guide
978-1-4267-5255-1

For more information, visit www.AdamHamilton.org.

Also by Adam Hamilton

The Journey
24 Hours That Changed the World
Forgiveness
Why?
When Christians Get It Wrong
Seeing Gray in a World of Black and White
Christianity's Family Tree

Selling Swimsuits in the Arctic
Christianity and World Religions
Confronting the Controversies
Making Love Last a Lifetime
Unleashing the Word
Leading Beyond the Walls
Final Words From the Cross

Adam Hamilton

The Way

40 Days of Reflection

Abingdon Press
Nashville

The Way:
40 Days of Reflection

Copyright © 2012 by Abingdon Press

All rights reserved.

This book is printed on acid-free paper.

ISBN 978-1-4267-5252-0

12 13 14 15 16 17 18 19 20—10 9 8 7 6 5 4 3 2 1

MANUFACTURED IN THE UNITED STATES OF AMERICA

Contents

Introduction

THE DEVOTIONAL you have in your hand is a companion to the book *The Way: Walking in the Footsteps of Jesus.* That book offers a more comprehensive study of the life of Jesus including maps, descriptions of the places Jesus walked, and reflections on the meaning of his life for our lives today. In a companion DVD, designed for small groups and individual use, I take readers to the Holy Land to see the places where Jesus walked.

I imagine this devotional being used during the season of Lent or another forty-day period of focused attention on the life of Jesus. The first six daily readings tie into the first chapter in the companion book; the next six daily readings tie into the second chapter; and so on. My suggestion is that you read chapter 1 of the book on Sunday, then use the corresponding devotional readings on the Monday through Saturday that follow. You'll find that the book and devotional, though based on the same passages of Scripture, present different insights. My hope is that they will complement one another.

Think of the devotional as I do—as though you and I were having an informal conversation over a cup of coffee. In each reading we'll consider a passage from the gospels and what that passages teaches us about walking as Christ's followers today. We'll begin where Mark's gospel begins, with Jesus' baptism, and we'll conclude with Jesus' final words after his resurrection.

I do have one suggestion that will enrich your use of this devotional: I have included just a few verses from each passage in the devotional, but my hope is that you will find the text in your Bible and read the day's story in its entirety. My comments will often draw upon insights from the rest of the passage.

I pray that these conversations will bless you as you read them. They have blessed me as I wrote them.

Adam Hamilton

Week One

BAPTISM AND TEMPTATION

The Jordan River and the Wilderness

At that time Jesus came from Nazareth in Galilee and was baptized by John in the Jordan. Just as Jesus was coming up out of the water, he saw heaven being torn open and the Spirit descending on him like a dove. And a voice came from heaven: "You are my Son, whom I love; with you I am well pleased." At once the Spirit sent him out into the wilderness, and he was in the wilderness forty days, being tempted by Satan. (Mark 1:9-13 NIV)

Monday

BAPTISM AND FORGIVENESS

John the baptizer appeared in the wilderness, proclaiming a baptism of repentance for the forgiveness of sins. And people from the whole Judean countryside and all the people of Jerusalem were going out to him, and were baptized by him in the river Jordan, confessing their sins. (Mark 1:4-5 NRSV)

THE JORDAN RIVER, where John was baptizing, was an eight-hour walk through the desert from Jerusalem. Yet Mark tells us that many from Jerusalem made the trek to hear John preach and to be immersed by him in the Jordan. Why did they walk eight hours, some more, to answer John's call to repent?

John dressed in the garments of a prophet. He spoke powerfully. People came believing that God had sent this man, and that his message was from God. He called the people to repent and to be baptized for the forgiveness of their sins. What John offered at the Jordan was God's forgiveness and a chance to begin anew. Which of us doesn't long for this at times?

She was in her thirties and had lived a hard life. She began attending our church, yearning for a new beginning. She had come to be baptized, and I spoke with her about the meaning of this act. In my tribe (Methodists), baptism has a kaleidoscope of meanings. Among these, it is a dramatic sign of God's grace and mercy—his willingness to wash us and make us new. It is an outward sign of God's forgiveness.

As she approached the baptistery she had tears in her eyes. She asked, "Pastor Adam, does God really forgive all that I've done? I've done a lot of terrible things." I assured her that as she came to God, repentant, he would forgive it all. And I reminded her that Christian baptism is a sign not only of God's forgiveness for sins in the past, but a promise of forgiveness when, in the future, we stumble and need his grace. And thus, with her baptism, she began a new life.

Do you ever feel a yearning for forgiveness and a new beginning? Every morning as I step into the shower, I remember my baptism and ask God to wash me and make me new. At times I feel a profound sense of my own sin and my longing for his grace. At other times I simply know that there are ways in which I have not lived up to his calling on my life. Either way, I recall with gratitude God's forgiveness and his claim upon my life.

If you have yet to be baptized, speak with your pastor about this profound act. If you have been baptized, remember your baptism each day as you bathe, inviting God, once again, to wash you and cover you by his grace.

Lord, in thought, word, and deed, by what I have done and what I have left undone, I have sinned against you and others. Remember the promise you made at my baptism, and wash me anew. I call upon the grace you offer us in Jesus Christ. Amen.

Tuesday

[And John said to them,] "Bear fruits worthy of repentance."... And the crowds asked him, "What then should we do?" In reply he said to them, "Whoever has two coats must share with anyone who has none; and whoever has food must do likewise." (Luke 3:8-11 NRSV)

REPENTANCE INVOLVES THE ENTIRE PERSON: head, heart, and hands. The word in Greek, *metanoia,* means literally to "think differently afterward" and signifies a change of thinking that leads to a change of heart that leads ultimately to a change in behavior. It is not enough, John said to the multitudes who came to be baptized, to step into the water. Repentance is accompanied by a change in life—there must be fruit born of repentance and baptism.

It is interesting to note that in Luke's gospel, when the people asked what this fruit looked like, all three of John's responses were economic in nature. Fruit worthy of repentance involved a person who had two coats sharing one with a person who had none (verse 11). For tax collectors, it was making sure not to overcharge people when collecting taxes (verse 13). And for soldiers, it was refusing to extort money through false accusations and being content with their pay (verse 14).

John's list wasn't comprehensive, but it was interesting nonetheless. If you and I are seeking to live as those who are repentant sinners—as those who wish to live for God—then we'll share with those in need, we'll be fair in our business dealings, and we'll be content with our pay.

My experience is that people who live this way—who are generous and giving, who seek to be honest and fair, and who are not focused on constantly yearning for more—are happier in life and usually more successful. Who do you admire more: people who are generous or people who are greedy? Who would you rather do business with: people who only look out for themselves or people who have your best interests at heart? Who would you rather have as a friend: people who are never content and slander others or people who are content with what they have and speak well of others?

Reed lives by John's list. A banker and a member of the church I serve, he's one of a thousand people I know like him. Reed carries his success with humility. He is genuinely interested in his clients and puts their needs before his own. And if he saw someone who needed a coat, he would give it without being asked. Reed isn't perfect, but to me he exhibits the economic fruit of repentance John called for.

Are you producing the fruits of repentance? Are you

regularly giving to help those in need? Are you fair and honest in all your dealings? Do you speak well of others? And are you cultivating contentment with what you have?

Lord, help me to produce fruit in keeping with repentance. Help me to be generous, honest, and content with what I have. In Jesus' name. Amen.

Wednesday

THE BAPTISM OF JESUS

Then Jesus came from Galilee to John at the Jordan, to be baptized by him. John would have prevented him, saying, "I need to be baptized by you, and do you come to me?" But Jesus answered him, "Let it be so now; for it is proper for us in this way to fulfill all righteousness." Then he consented. And when Jesus had been baptized, just as he came up from the water, suddenly the heavens were opened to him and he saw the Spirit of God descending like a dove and alighting on him. And a voice from heaven said, "This is my Son, the Beloved, with whom I am well pleased." (Matthew 3:13-17 NRSV)

JESUS WAS INTENTIONAL ABOUT beginning his public ministry by coming to his cousin, John, to be baptized. This was a kind of ordination and unveiling for Jesus.

But why would Jesus be baptized? Why would he need

a "baptism of repentance for the forgiveness of sins?" This is a question Christians have wrestled with since the first Gospels were written. Matthew raises the question for us by citing John's words to Jesus: "I need to be baptized by you, and you come to me?" (Matthew 3:14 NRSV).

In choosing to be baptized, Jesus was identifying fully with humanity. He stood publicly with those who felt alienated from God and in need of grace. He waded into the water with the broken, the guilty, and those who felt far from God. This was a foreshadowing of what he would do in his ministry, when he befriended sinners and tax collectors, and ultimately when he died on the cross.

I'm reminded of Joan Osborne's 1995 song, "One of Us," that famously asked, "What if God was one of us / Just a slob like one of us."[1] When Jesus stepped into the Jordan River to be baptized, he was "just a slob like one of us." He was showing himself to be the "Son of Man," a phrase that appears eighty-one times in the Gospels to describe Jesus.

But even as Jesus showed himself to be the Son of Man, the heavens opened, the Spirit descended, and he heard the voice of God say, "This is my Son, the Beloved, with whom I am well pleased" (Matthew 3:17 NRSV). He was not only the Son of Man. He was the *beloved* Son of God.

Jesus was called "Beloved" by the Father. The Greek word is *agapetos,* and it is a term of great affection. I think of the love I have for my daughters and my wife, who are beloved to me. The apostles came to use the word as a way of addressing their fellow Christians. Again and again in the letters of the New Testament, the apostles addressed Christians as "Beloved." Who are they beloved by? They, and we, are beloved by God.

We believe that in our baptism God claims us as his beloved children, just as he did with Jesus, his only begotten Son. When we remember our baptisms, we remember our identity, and we remember that God has a deep affection for all of us. We are God's beloved children.

As you reflect upon Jesus' baptism, remember his humility in choosing to identify with broken and sinful people. Remember the Father's claim, in his baptism, that Jesus was his beloved son. But pause for a moment to remember your own baptism. Know that God has claimed you as his beloved child.

Jesus, thank you for identifying with our human brokenness—that we might identify with your divine sonship. Help me to believe that I really am one of the Father's beloved. Amen.

Thursday

TEMPTED BY FOOD

Then Jesus was led up by the Spirit into the wilderness to be tempted by the devil. He fasted forty days and forty nights, and afterwards he was famished. The tempter came and said to him, "If you are the Son of God, command these stones to become loaves of bread." But he answered, "It is written, 'One does not live by bread alone, but by every word that comes from the mouth of God.'" (Matthew 4:1-4 NRSV)

I WEIGHED MYSELF THIS MORNING. I was one pound heavier than yesterday. How did that happen? Ugh! It's a constant battle in my life. Do I eat that extra piece of pizza? Do I grab a handful of dark chocolate peanut M&Ms from the jar by my desk? Do I super-size it, or accept the smallish regular size? And yes, I'll take my cake *à la mode*.

I struggle daily with the temptation of food. The percentage of Americans who are overweight tells me that I'm not alone.

Immediately after hearing the voice of the Father saying he was God's beloved son, Jesus left John and the Jordan behind and made his way to the wilderness to fast and pray for forty days. The wilderness of Judea is breathtakingly beautiful. It is a desert made up of mountains and hills and hundreds ravines cut by rivers that flow when the rains come. Caves line the walls of the ravines and the sides of the mountains. Once, thousands of monks lived in those caves; the few monks who still live there can be found in one of the handful of monasteries built into those mountainsides.

Jesus came to the desert to fast for forty days, just as Moses and Elijah had done centuries before him. Fasting is difficult because food is our most basic of needs.

Our brains are wired to be looking constantly for the next meal. Fasting is a way of redirecting our focus from food to God. It is a way of reminding ourselves that we "do not live by bread alone, but by every word that comes from the mouth of God."

The devil came to Jesus near the end of his fast. I doubt that the devil appeared in physical form; instead, he probably came as he does when tempting and testing us, through a whisper or a thought planted in our brain that will not let us go. The temptation was for Jesus to break his fast and eat. It was food the tempter tested him with, just as he had tested Adam and Eve in the Garden long before.

Interpreters have seen much more in this temptation. The devil twice remarked, "If you are the Son of God…" as if Jesus' struggle was whether he really believed what God had said at the Jordan River. This is precisely how the devil tempted Adam and Eve: "Did God really say not to eat the fruit of this tree?" (Genesis 3:1, paraphrase). Perhaps Jesus' real temptation was to use his power to alleviate the hunger he felt, just as later he was tempted to use his power to avoid the cross. Maybe the devil was planting a seed in his mind that if he could turn stones to bread, he might also win followers while bypassing the cross. All of these thoughts may have been a part of the temptation that day.

Ultimately, as I read this temptation, I remember that Jesus was tempted by the very thing I struggle with each day. He had the self-control to say no to the devil's whispers, to neither break his fast nor use his powers for self-preservation. Jesus reminded himself and the devil that we don't live by bread alone. We live by the words that proceed from the mouth of God. This, in the end, is the point of fasting.

Jesus, thank you for revealing the story of your temptations to the disciples, who shared those stories with us. It is good to know that you, too, struggled with temptation. Help me in my struggles with the tempter. Amen.

Friday

Then the devil took him to the holy city and placed him on the pinnacle of the temple, saying to him, "If you are the Son of God, throw yourself down; for it is written, 'He will command his angels concerning you,' and 'On their hands they will bear you up, so that you will not dash your foot against a stone.'" Jesus said to him, "Again it is written, 'Do not put the Lord your God to the test.'" (Matthew 4:5-7 NRSV)

I LOVE TO BE DARING—not too daring, but just a bit. I like to ski, fast. I enjoy riding my motorcycle with the wind at my face and the pavement under my feet. I like to hike in the mountains, getting fairly close to the edge.

I enjoy taking mission trips to developing nations, hiking alone with a backpack across Israel, and traveling to retrace Moses' life even as Egypt is experiencing turmoil.

These things all come with risks. I try to calculate those risks and minimize them by, for example, wearing a helmet when riding my motorcycle or avoiding trips to locations that are too dangerous. But I'm also aware that there is some element of risk in almost everything we do. It's impossible to avoid completely. Every time I get in my car to drive, there is risk involved.

Do I believe that because I am a Christian, a pastor, a tither or because I carry a Bible in my back pocket every day, nothing bad will happen to me? No. Bad things happen to Christians, to pastors, and to tithers.

I knew a man who died while showing off driving his very fast car. His friends were angry, wanting to know how God could have let it happen. The man was in the prime of life, was the father of two children, and he was a follower of Jesus. But the laws of physics still applied.

This is part of what I think the devil meant when he

suggested that Jesus jump from the pinnacle of the Temple. The devil even quoted one of the beautiful Psalms of promise: "Jump, Jesus, for the Scripture says he protects those he loves, and he'll protect you" (Matthew 4:6, paraphrase). In jumping, Jesus could prove to himself, and to all in the Temple courts, that he really was the Son of God. But Jesus responded, "It is also written, 'Do not put the Lord your God to the test.'" In other words, even Jesus wasn't expecting God to suspend the laws of physics if he jumped.

Jesus, at times I've been confused by the tragedies that happen in our world. I want you to suspend the laws of nature and protect those I love, and yet I see that even you did not expect this from the Father. Help me to live wisely, and to trust that in living and dying I will belong to you. Amen.

Saturday

MONEY AND POWER

Again, the devil took him to a very high mountain and showed him all the kingdoms of the world and their splendor; and he said to him, "All these I will give you, if you will fall down and worship me." Jesus said to him, "Away with you, Satan! for it is written, 'Worship the Lord your God, and serve only him.'" (Matthew 4:8-10 NRSV)

IN APRIL OF 2011, A SEVENTEEN-year-old Chinese high school student named Wang made news around the world after it was discovered that he had sold one of his kidneys to buy an iPhone and an iPad. His mother later reported that, in fact, Wang had received $3,500 for his kidney, and only after receiving the money did he decide to buy the technology devices. Nevertheless, Wang's story became a kind of parable about confused values and the lure of money. Five people were arrested for luring Wang to sell his kidney, including the surgeon who harvested it.

We are shocked by such stories of misguided and potentially deadly acts in pursuit of more, and yet, aren't many of us in a way guilty of similar acts? I think of the economic crisis of 2008 that unfolded first in the United States and then around the world, which continues to shape our economy years later. Americans mortgaged their futures to buy iPads and iPhones, big screen televisions, and mini-mansions. Even those not living beyond their means benefited from increases in the stock market and housing market that resulted from unbridled spending.

Jesus, too, was tempted by wealth. The fact that he knew its allure allowed him to teach powerfully on the subject. He taught his disciples that one's life does not consist of the abundance of possessions. He preached that we cannot serve both God and money. He taught and modeled for his disciples that "the one who would be great among you must become your servant." In this temptation, Jesus came face to face with the lure of wealth and power and said, "No! For it is written, 'Worship the Lord your God and serve only him'" (Matthew 4:10 NRSV).

In what ways do you struggle with materialism? How much energy do you devote to "storing up treasures on earth?" Jesus was right to associate this temptation with false worship. Without even realizing it, we can make the desire for wealth into an idol.

Jesus knew this temptation, and he sought to show us a better way. Wealth is not evil in and of itself. But, Paul rightly wrote, "the love of money is a root of all kinds of evil" (1 Timothy 6:10 NRSV). Paul offered the antidote when he advised us to "do good, to be rich in good works, generous, and ready to share, thus storing up…the treasure of a good foundation for the future, so that [we] may take hold of the life that really is life" (1 Timothy 6:18-19 NRSV).

Lord, you know what it is to be tempted by the desire for riches. Help me to say no to the false gods of wealth and power, and instead to worship and serve only you. Help me to be generous and ready to share. Amen.

Week Two

THE HEALING MINISTRY

Capernaum

Now when Jesus heard that John had been arrested, he withdrew to Galilee. He left Nazareth and made his home in Capernaum by the sea. (Matthew 4:12-13 NRSV)

They went to Capernaum; and when the sabbath came, he entered the synagogue and taught. They were astounded at his teaching, for he taught them as one having authority, and not as the scribes. Just then there was in their synagogue a man with an unclean spirit, and he cried out, "What have you to do with us, Jesus of Nazareth? Have you come to destroy us? I know who you are, the Holy One of God." But Jesus rebuked him, saying, "Be silent, and come out of him!" (Mark 1:21-25 NRSV)

As soon as they left the synagogue, they entered the house of Simon and Andrew, with James and John. Now Simon's mother-

in-law was in bed with a fever, and they told him about her at once. He came and took her by the hand and lifted her up. Then the fever left her, and she began to serve them. That evening, at sunset, they brought to him all who were sick or possessed with demons. (Mark 1:29-32 NRSV)

Monday

Nazareth Rejects Jesus

When he came to Nazareth, where he had been brought up, he went to the synagogue on the sabbath day, as was his custom…. They got up, drove him out of the town, and led him to the brow of the hill on which their town was built, so that they might hurl him off the cliff. (Luke 4:16, 29 NRSV)

JESUS HAD JUST RETURNED HOME after a two- to three-month journey that included his baptism by John and forty days of fasting in the wilderness. On the Sabbath, he entered the small synagogue in Nazareth to preach what may have been his first sermon in his hometown. Jesus' family was present, along with those who had grown up with him and those who had watched him grow up. Jesus all but announced that he was the Messiah, come to bring good news to the poor. He went on to make clear that he would minister not only to Jews but also to Gentiles.

It was Jesus' willingness to minister with Gentiles that most upset those in the synagogue. Pondering this, I could not help but think of politics in America. In some churches, a pastor who admitted voting Democrat would be run out of the congregation, while in others, a pastor who admitted voting Republican would suffer the same fate. Our convictions about who is in and who is out, about who is loved by God and who isn't, often run deep.

Jesus' reference to Gentiles' receiving the grace of God infuriated many in the synagogue. By the time he was finished, the men of the synagogue were so angry that they dragged him outside and planned to throw him off a cliff! Had that been my first experience preaching in my own hometown, I think it also would have been my last experience preaching. I might have given up.

This would not be the last time Jesus was rejected. The religious leaders would reject him again and again. Even many of his followers would turn away. At times people would beg him to leave town. One of his disciples would betray him. The others would deny knowing him. Ultimately he would be crucified.

Rejection is a part of life. We all know it from time to time. After experiencing rejection, there comes the temptation to give up. It hurts, and we don't like being hurt, so we choose never again to say or do the things that caused us to be rejected.

There are times when our rejection comes because we missed the mark. In those cases we have to learn from rejection, allowing it to be a springboard for getting it right the next time.

But there are other times when what we said or did was right, yet it led to our rejection. Every great leader in the Bible and throughout history knew this type of rejection. What made these leaders great was that they refused to give up.

When you have been criticized, persecuted, or rejected for saying and doing what is right, you must follow the example of Jesus who, when he was rejected, refused to give up.

Lord, thank you for persevering in the face of rejection. Help me to learn from rejection and to grow through it. When rejection comes because I've said or done the right thing, give me the strength and courage to not give up. Amen.

Tuesday

EXORCISING DEMONS

He went down to Capernaum, a city in Galilee, and was teaching them on the sabbath. They were astounded at his teaching, because he spoke with authority. In the synagogue there was a man who had the spirit of an unclean demon, and he cried out with a loud voice, "Let us alone! What have you to do with us, Jesus of Nazareth? Have you come to destroy us? I know who you are, the Holy One of God." But Jesus rebuked him, saying, "Be silent, and come out of him!" (Luke 4:31-35 NRSV)

JESUS LEFT NAZARETH AND MADE his way to the lakefront village of Capernaum, on the Sea of Galilee. There he attempted to teach and preach in the synagogue, as he had at Nazareth. But what a difference! The people "were astounded at his teaching."

While teaching, Jesus was confronted by a man who was possessed by a demon. This was the first of many times in the Gospel record in which Jesus encountered the demonic. What we find in these encounters is that the demons were always afraid of Jesus, and they had no power compared to his. In Luke 4:34, a man possessed by a demon shouted at the top of his voice, "Jesus of Nazareth, have you come to destroy us? I know who you are, the Holy One of God" (NRSV).

Recently I sat down with a young man struggling with what the doctors diagnosed as obsessive-compulsive disorder (OCD). He was having thoughts that God did not want him to sit in a certain chair, or to drive on a certain road, or to walk into a certain place, and if he disobeyed, he believed he was betraying Christ and serving the devil. This was an otherwise healthy, successful, and intelligent young man.

The OCD was using his spirituality to rob him of life. I suggested that the OC thoughts were destructive and in fact were the antithesis of the freedom Christ intended him to have. In this sense his illness was demonic—demonic being the opposite of Christ's way. I said that I did not know if the voices he was hearing were merely his own, shaped by OCD, or if there was a spiritual entity behind them. Either way, the stories of Jesus' exorcism of demons could be helpful.

I reminded the young man about the story of the demon-possessed man in the synagogue at Capernaum, and how the demon was silenced when Jesus said, "Be still!" Then the demon left when Jesus said, "Come out!" I suggested that, in addition to receiving therapy and medicine, the young man should say to the voice he was hearing, "I know you are lying to me. In the name of Jesus Christ, leave me alone!" Several weeks ago I heard back from the young man, who told me this approach had provided a degree of relief from his OCD that medication and therapy alone had not provided.

When I have thoughts that I know are not of God—such as temptations, fears, or ideas that would lead me astray—I speak aloud to the devil, and perhaps to myself, "In the name of Jesus Christ, leave me alone!" Whether the thoughts are the whispers of demons, or merely the dark side of my own psyche, they are almost always silenced when I command them to leave in the name of Jesus.

Lord Jesus, in your presence the demons were silenced. When you said, "flee" they were forced to flee. Set me free from the voices that would lead me away from you. Help me to walk in freedom and joy. Protect me from the evil one. Amen.

Wednesday

THE GENTLE HEALER

After leaving the synagogue he entered Simon's house. Now Simon's mother-in-law was suffering from a high fever, and they asked him about her. Then he stood over her and rebuked the fever, and it left her. Immediately she got up and began to serve them.

As the sun was setting, all those who had any who were sick with various kinds of diseases brought them to him; and he laid his hands on each of them and cured them. (Luke 4:38-40 NRSV)

IN THE COMPANION BOOK TO this devotional, I describe Simon's house in Capernaum, which appears to have been converted to a church during the early centuries of the Christian faith. In the DVD, I take viewers to see the ruins of this home and the church that was later built over it. This home was likely the house where Jesus stayed when he was in Capernaum.

Upon entering the house following his first Sabbath service in Capernaum, Jesus found Simon's mother suffering from a high fever. Have you suffered from a high fever? I recently had my appendix removed because it was on the verge of rupturing. The night, before finally going to the doctor, I lay in bed, shaking and suffering with a high fever. The fever continued after surgery, keeping me in the hospital for several days. Though my illness was relatively minor compared to many, by the third night I was more than ready to be done with it and to sleep in my own bed.

That day in Capernaum, as Jesus stood over Simon's mother-in-law, he told the fever to leave, and with his words the infection in her body was destroyed. Her fever dissipated, and she got up and began to care for Jesus and the guests. I love this: Jesus spoke and the bacteria were banished—the virus vanished.

That night, people from around the countryside brought their sick to Simon's house, and Jesus touched each of them and healed them. He stayed up all night long healing them. This episode tells us, among other things, that Jesus was filled with compassion for the sick.

Today, Jesus' primary instrument of healing is still through human touch, by doctors and nurses and physical therapists. Before going in for surgery on my appendix, I asked the surgeon if I could pray for him. I took his hand, thanked him for his compassion and care for the sick, and then prayed, "Lord, thank you for Dr. McCrosky. I pray that you would use him to bring healing to my body. Bless him and help him as he seeks to help me. In Jesus' name, Amen." In the end he removed my appendix, treated my infection, and three days later I was home and feeling great. God used him as an agent of healing.

Those in the medical professions—doctors, nurses, hospital technicians, and therapists—all follow in the footsteps of Jesus through the work that they do.

The stories of Christ's healing ministry point to his compassion for the sick. When you are sick, know that he is always near. And pray for your doctors and nurses, because they are the instruments he uses most often to bring healing to our bodies.

Lord, grant me compassion for others when they are sick. Thank you for doctors and nurses and for all who work in the medical professions. Bless them in the work that they do. Amen.

Thursday

When he returned to Capernaum after some days, it was reported that he was at home. So many gathered around that there was no longer room for them, not even in front of the door; and he was speaking the word to them. Then some people came, bringing to him a paralyzed man, carried by four of them. And when they could not bring him to Jesus because of the crowd, they removed the roof above him; and after having dug through it, they let down the mat on which the paralytic lay. When Jesus saw their faith, he said to the paralytic, "Son, your sins are forgiven."
(Mark 2:1-5 NRSV)

IN THIS ACCOUNT, MARK NOTES that Jesus was "at home" in Capernaum. Once again, as had happened that first night in Capernaum, Jesus was ministering in a house, likely Simon's home where he was staying. The houses were relatively small, and there were perhaps twenty or thirty people surrounding him as he taught, with more standing in the doorway and at the windows. So, when the friends of a paralyzed man brought him on a stretcher to be touched and healed by Jesus, they could see that there was no getting into the house.

Some friends would have given up, saying, "We'll have to bring you to Jesus another time," but not these friends. Refusing to take "no" for an answer, they climbed to the roof of Simon's house, hoisting their paralyzed friend up with them and intending to lower him through the roof. Luke tells us that the roof consisted of tiles. Mark tells us, in the Greek, that they dug through the roof, which would imply a roof made of mud and reed or palm branches. In either case, these men were determined that Jesus would touch their friend, and they were willing to tear the roof off Simon's house to see that it happened.

Can you imagine the boisterous Simon Peter looking up as dust began to fall from the ceiling, then seeing the four men pulling off the roof to lower their friend? I can imagine him roaring in anger, "What in the name of Abraham are you doing to my house!?" But I picture Jesus reaching out his hand to calm Peter down.

The men lowered their friend before Jesus. Mark tells us, "Seeing their faith, he spoke to the paralytic" and healed him. In other words, the man was healed not because of his own faith, but due to the faith Jesus saw in his friends!

Everyone needs stretcher bearers like these—friends who will carry you when you are at your weakest, friends who not only will pray for you but will do whatever it takes to help you get back on your feet. In my experience, the only way to have such stretcher-bearers is to be a stretcher-bearer like that for someone else.

Who are your stretcher-bearers? Whose stretcher-bearer are you? Investing in them could change your life. It did for a man in Capernaum.

Lord, help me to be a stretcher-bearer for others—to give the time and energy to care for them and carry them when they need it most. Help me to be open to the care of others in my time of need. Amen.

Friday

After Jesus had finished all his sayings in the hearing of the people, he entered Capernaum. A centurion there had a slave whom he valued highly, and who was ill and close to death. When he heard about Jesus, he sent some Jewish elders to him, asking him to come and heal his slave. When they came to Jesus, they appealed to him earnestly, saying, "He is worthy of having you do this for him, for he loves our people, and it is he who built our synagogue for us." And Jesus went with them, but when he was not far from the house, the centurion sent friends to say to him, "Lord, do not trouble yourself, for I am not worthy to have you come under my roof; therefore I did not presume to come to you. But only speak the word, and let my servant be healed." (Luke 7:1-7 NRSV)

A CENTURION WAS A ROMAN soldier, an officer who commanded 60 to 100 soldiers. As for the particular centurion in today's Scripture, some have suggested that he was retired. He seems to have been a man of some means, having built the synagogue in Capernaum for the Jewish people. (He may have donated the funds or procured them from Rome.) In the DVD that is available for *The Way,* I show you the ruins of a later synagogue built atop the synagogue this centurion had constructed.

The centurion's highly valued servant was near death, so the centurion asked the town elders to seek Jesus' help. Jesus showed no hesitancy about going to heal the servant of a centurion in the Roman occupying army. Nor did he appear hesitant to enter the home of the centurion.

As Jesus was on his way, the soldier sent his friends to say, "Lord, do not trouble yourself to come to my house. I'm not worthy for you to enter my home. Just say the word and my servant will be healed." Jesus found this remarkable.

While many Jews did not yet understand or believe that Jesus was the Messiah, this man recognized Jesus' ability to heal and his authority over illness, even at some distance. Jesus noted, "I tell you, not even in Israel have I found such faith" (Luke 7:9 NRSV.) Jesus gave the word, and the man's servant was healed.

Just a few verses earlier, in Luke 6, Jesus taught his followers to love their enemies and do good to those who mistreated them (Luke 6:28-38). In the story of the centurion, Jesus demonstrated what he had just taught and what he would teach again and again: that his was a call not to take up arms against Romans, but to win them over by acts of kindness and mercy.

We're not in a land under occupation, so who today is the equivalent of the Roman soldier needing our help? Could it be someone of the opposing political party, a Republican or Democrat? Could it be a person of an entirely different faith from our own? Walking in the footsteps of Jesus means ministering to those who need us, even if they appear to be an outsider or an enemy.

Lord, you dropped what you were doing to heal the servant of your people's enemy. You did not see him as your enemy but as someone who needed you. Help me to demonstrate love and care for those who are outside my social group, particularly for those who might naturally be considered my enemies. Amen.

Saturday

When they came to the house of the leader of the synagogue, he saw a commotion, people weeping and wailing loudly. When he had entered, he said to them, "Why do you make a commotion and weep? The child is not dead but sleeping." And they laughed at him. Then he put them all outside, and took the child's father and mother and those who were with him, and went in where the child was. He took her by the hand and said to her, "Talitha cum," which means, "Little girl, get up!" And immediately the girl got up and began to walk about (she was twelve years of age). (Mark 5:38-42 NRSV)

IN TODAY'S STORY, THE LAY LEADER of the synagogue was a man named Jairus. His twelve-year-old daughter was very sick at home, and he had fallen at Jesus' feet, begging Jesus to come and heal his daughter. Jesus immediately left with Jairus, but while they were on the way home, friends came to say that the daughter had died. Jesus turned to Jairus and said, "Do not fear, only believe" (Mark 5:36 NRSV).

Jesus took Jairus, his wife, and a few disciples to the girl's room and asked the mourners to leave. He took the girl by the hand and spoke, commanding her to get up, and immediately she was well! What a remarkable scene.

This was the second instance in the Gospels of Jesus restoring someone to life. The first, recorded in Luke 7:11-17, took place in a town called Nain, where Jesus had seen a widow grieving the death of her son. His heart had gone out to the widow, and he had stopped the funeral procession, saying to her dead son, "Young man, get up!" The boy sat up, very much alive (Luke 7:14-15).

A third incident of Jesus raising someone from the grave is found in John 11, where Jesus was moved to tears at the grief of Lazarus' sister. Jesus went to the tomb and shouted, "Lazarus, come out!" To everyone's astonishment, Lazarus stumbled out of the grave (John 11:43-44).

These stories have two things in common. First, in each instance Jesus was moved with compassion for those who were grieving. He knew that on the other side of death was life, and that those who have died live again; nevertheless, he was deeply moved by the sorrow of those who mourned. Second, Jesus spoke to the people who had died, and by his word their bodies were reanimated. The biochemical processes of death and decay were instantly reversed, and their souls reentered their bodies—all at the sound of his voice.

Some years ago, a twelve-year-old girl in our congregation named Katie died of a rare disease. Her mother and father, like Jairus and his wife, loved their daughter very much. I shared this story from Mark's gospel at Katie's funeral. It served as a reminder of Christ's compassion for grieving parents. But this story, and the other stories of resurrection in the Gospels, point to the hope we have in Christ. Katie died at 8:30 a.m. on a Sunday morning. I'm convinced that on that day, at that very hour, Jesus said to her, *"Talitha cum"* ("Little girl, get up!").

Jesus is deeply moved by our grief. And he is "the resurrection and the life." Those who believe in him, "though they die, yet shall they live." In the words of Charles Wesley's famous hymn, "He speaks, and listening to his voice, new life the dead receive!"[2]

Lord, I remember now those whom I have loved and lost to death. Thank you for the Gospel stories in which you spoke and people rose to life. I trust that my loved ones are with you and that one day I will see you, and them, face to face. Amen.

Week Three

Proclaiming the Kingdom

The Mountains

When Jesus saw the crowds, he went up the mountain; and after he sat down, his disciples came to him. Then he began to speak, and taught them. (Matthew 5:1-2a)

"Everyone then who hears these words of mine and acts on them will be like a wise man who built his house on rock. The rain fell, the floods came, and the winds blew and beat on that house, but it did not fall, because it had been founded on rock. And everyone who hears these words of mine and does not act on them will be like a foolish man who built his house on sand. The rain fell, and the floods came, and the winds blew and beat against that house, and it fell—and great was its fall!" Now when Jesus had finished saying these things, the crowds were astounded at his teaching, for he taught them as one having authority, and not as their scribes. (Matthew 7:24-29 NRSV)

Monday

> *"You are the light of the world. A city built on a hill cannot be hid. No one after lighting a lamp puts it under the bushel basket, but on the lampstand, and it gives light to all in the house. In the same way, let your light shine before others, so that they may see your good works and give glory to your Father in heaven."* *(Matthew 5:14-16)*

THIS WEEK WE'LL TURN TO some of the teachings of Jesus, starting with selected readings from the Sermon on the Mount.

* * *

Jesus ascended one of the mountains that borders the Sea of Galilee, accompanied by his disciples and a large crowd of people. There he began to lay out the mission, ethics, and spirituality of the Kingdom of God. When I read the Sermon on the Mount, it represents for me the highest ideals I hope to live by. I've found it particularly helpful to pray the Sermon on the Mount. I focus on one brief section, like the one above, and then I pray that God will help me to live the command I've just read.

On the hillsides surrounding the Sea of Galilee there were, in Jesus day, scattered villages. Each home had one or more small oil lamps to light it at night. One oil lamp from one home might have been hard to see from a distance. But when an entire village of people were trimming their lamps at night, it could be seen across the lake—it could not be hidden.

In our passage, Jesus used the plural form of the word *you*. He said, in essence, "You, together, are the light of the world. You are meant to be like a village on a hill." Jesus was speaking not only about how we should live our lives individually; ultimately he was describing the community of his followers—in other words, the church.

But how do we let our light shine? We do it by our good works. In this context, the Greek word for "good"—*kalos*—may also be translated as "beautiful." We are to demonstrate beautiful deeds that draw others to God.

There was a time when the church I serve was known for its size. People would say, "Oh, that's the big church." But ten years ago we began asking, "What would happen if we became known not for the size of our congregation but the depth of our concern for the community? What if we actually lived up to Jesus' words in the Sermon on the Mount and sought to shine Christ's light through beautiful deeds of loving kindness?" We increased our efforts at serving the community, at sending our members to care for others, and in our work supporting those in need. Today, every member is called and expected to serve.

I remember, as a child, occasionally seeing giant searchlights in the sky at night, announcing the grand opening of a business or some special event. If we were in the car we would beg our parents to take us to the light, so we could see what was going on. This is the picture I have of the church as Jesus envisioned it. Every member should be working individually and together to demonstrate such beautiful deeds that others are drawn to the church and to her Christ.

Jesus, help me so that the doing of beautiful deeds might be a daily rhythm of my life. Lead my church so that together we might be "a city set upon a hill that cannot be hidden." Amen.

Tuesday

I tell you, unless your righteousness exceeds that of the scribes and Pharisees, you will never enter the kingdom of heaven. (Matthew 5:20 NRSV)

THE SERMON ON THE MOUNT SEEMS, at so many points, impossible to live. It must have seemed the same to Jesus' first hearers. The Pharisees were focused on purity before God. The name *Pharisee* means "set apart" or "separated," and they sought to distinguish themselves by the lengths to which they would go in being pious. How could anyone's righteousness exceed that of the Pharisees?

Some have felt that the point of the Sermon on the Mount was to offer an impossible picture of righteousness, so we would be led naturally to recognize our need for a Savior. Perhaps. I'm more inclined to see it as capturing an ideal that is always beyond where we are and yet offers a vision of piety for which we are meant to strive.

The piety described by Jesus involves more than just obeying the letter of the Law; he asked that our hearts and motives and words be holy. Consider what Jesus taught in Matthew 5: The Law says not to murder; I say don't speak with anger or hatred toward another. The Law says not to commit adultery; I say don't look at another with adultery in your heart. The Law allows divorce; I say that vows were meant to be kept. The Law says not to break an oath; I say you shouldn't need to swear an oath, and your word should always be your bond. The Law says you can seek retributive justice—an eye for an eye and a tooth for a tooth; I say you should turn the other cheek when wronged. Common wisdom says to love your neighbor and hate your enemy; I say to love your enemy and pray for those who persecute you.

I don't claim to live up to these words of Jesus. I sometimes speak in anger. I occasionally find lust knocking at the door of my heart. I've stretched the truth, and I've found it hard to turn the other cheek. At times I haven't wanted to pray for, much less love, my enemies. But while I don't perfectly live up to these teachings of Jesus, his words represent an ideal to which I strive. They define the person I want to be, and they often form the words of my prayer: "Lord, forgive me for falling short of your will, and help me become the person you described in the Sermon on the Mount."

Perhaps you could pick a section from the Sermon on the Mount that describes something you struggle with, and begin to pray that God will help you become the person God desires you to be.

The Pharisees excelled at following rules and displaying outward purity. Jesus called us to have hearts that are pure—inward purity—and to practice acts of love, mercy, and faithfulness. This is what it means to have a righteousness that exceeds the scribes and the Pharisees.

Lord, I fall short of the ideals you set out in the Sermon on the Mount, but they do reflect the person I wish to be. Help me, by your Spirit, to become the person you long for me to be. Amen.

Wednesday

HIDE YOUR GOOD WORKS?

Beware of practicing your piety before others in order to be seen by them; for then you have no reward from your Father in heaven. So whenever you give alms, do not sound a trumpet before you, as the hypocrites do in the synagogues and in the streets, so that they may be praised by others. Truly I tell you, they have received their reward. (Matthew 6:1-2 NRSV)

IN MATTHEW 5:14-16, JESUS TOLD his followers to let others see their good works and thus give glory to God. But in the very next chapter, Matthew 6, Jesus told his disciples not to practice acts of piety before others in order to be seen by them. Which is it? Do we do our good works before others, or do we hide our good works?

The difference between these two commands is in the motivation. In the first case, beautiful works are done for others, both as an act of obedience to God and as a way of leading others to him. (Jesus noted that by our good works, others were meant to "give glory to their Father in heaven.") But in the second case, Jesus warned against doing acts of piety with the aim of being praised by others. The difference is who is intended to get the glory: God or you?

Jesus followed up the second command by naming three deeds of piety that his followers might be tempted to practice in a way that draws attention and praise to themselves. He noted that the "hypocrites" practice deeds of piety in this way. *Hypocrite,* in Greek, signifies an actor on a stage—a pretender—and Jesus almost always used this term to refer to the religious leaders. The three acts that Jesus named: giving to the poor, praying, and fasting.

Why did Jesus feel the need to warn his disciples about drawing attention to themselves? Because he knew that they, and we, would struggle with this temptation. There is something inside us that wants affirmation, and when we've done something good, we want to be noticed. But somehow the very act of doing these things in order to be praised by others undermines the original purpose of the acts, which was to bless others and glorify God.

Do you struggle with the desire to be noticed for your piety? Do you find yourself wanting to tell others when you are fasting, or what you are fasting from? Do you ever secretly want others to know that you made a sizable donation to a particular cause? When you pray, do you find yourself wanting others to know it? I'm embarrassed and ashamed to say that at times in my Christian life, I have struggled with each of these desires.

Jesus told his followers to give in secret, to pray in a place where no one listened, to fast without telling anyone, and "your Father who sees in secret will reward you" (Matthew 6:4 NRSV). Cultivating the habit of secrecy, anonymity, and deflecting the glory to God is a part of spiritual maturity. In the end we may not be able to hide our beautiful deeds, but we can work to do them for God's glory and not our own.

Lord, please forgive me for the times when I was one of the hypocrites, doing spiritual things with motives that were not spiritual. Help me to resist the urge to be noticed and affirmed by anyone but you. May my life be lived for your glory and not my own. Amen.

Thursday

MONEY AND THE KINGDOM OF GOD

Where your treasure is, there your heart will be also...No one can serve two masters; for a slave will either hate the one and love the other, or be devoted to the one and despise the other. You cannot serve God and wealth... strive first for the kingdom of God and his righteousness, and all these things will be given to you as well. (Matthew 6:21, 24, 33 NRSV)

MONEY WAS A TOPIC JESUS FREQUENTLY addressed in the Gospels.

Jesus personally knew the temptation to bypass God's mission in order to have more money, yet he resisted. He knew that it was human nature to hoard and store rather than to give and share. He knew that while we claim that God is King in our lives, we often live as though cash is king. He knew that we human beings worry about money. For all these reasons, Jesus regularly addressed this topic.

It is so easy for us to believe that money and material things will bring us happiness. To some degree, at times, they do—but only to a point. I recently bought a new car. I'd been looking, researching, dreaming, and saving for several years in anticipation of the purchase. I was excited when I picked up my new Mustang, but I noticed that within a few days the feeling wore off. Several weeks later, when someone left a large ding in my door, I had to remind myself, "It's only a car."

I went to visit a member of my church yesterday. She was nearing the end of a battle with cancer. Her husband, children, and good friend were sitting around her. She said to me and to them, "It seems so clear to me right now that houses and cars and things really don't matter. The only things that matters are the people I love, the memories we share, and our faith in God—what he's done for us and what we do in living for him. None of the rest really matters."

So many people devote their lives to the amassing of money and the acquisition of things. It is the American way. But Jesus reminded us that there can be only one king on the throne of our hearts. We can only have one "most important thing."

A friend I know received a windfall this year. He had an investment that left him with $500,000 in income that he had not expected. He made a list of what he would do with the money. His first decision was to give $150,000 to his church and to projects benefiting low-income people. His second was to set aside enough to pay taxes on it. His third was to help a couple of family members. Finally he set aside money for retirement. Only after doing all of these things did he spend any of it on things he and his wife might enjoy. He noted that the money he gave away was the most rewarding thing he did with his windfall.

What is your relationship with money and possessions? What do you treasure? Are you seeking first the Kingdom of God?

Lord, you know the temptation of wealth and possessions. I confess that there have been times when I did not seek first your kingdom; when money, possessions, and the acquiring of them took greater priority in my heart. Forgive me, and help me to treasure you and your kingdom above all else. Amen.

Friday

THE RULE

"In everything do to others as you would have them do to you;
for this is the law and the prophets." (Matthew 7:12 NRSV)

SOMEWHERE ALONG THE WAY, even those who were not
raised going to church were probably taught the Golden
Rule: "Do unto others…." Jesus was not the first person
to express this idea, but he was known for an important
restatement of the rule. Others had taught, "Don't do to
others what you would not want done to you." Jesus'
command included that idea but went far beyond it: "In
everything, do to others as you would have them do to
you." He followed the command with an amazing statement: "This is the law and the prophets."

Jesus' restatement of the command summarized the ethical requirements of God; that is why we memorize the statement as children. We often leave out the words "In everything," but I think these are important. In every conversation, every business transaction, every interaction, every decision—in everything, "do to others as you would have them do to you."

A lifelong Christian, discovering that his car needs two thousand dollars of repairs, trades the car in without telling the dealer about the needed repairs. A women's Bible study leader regularly belittles her husband. A leader in the church feels it is his "Christian duty" to forward political e-mails without checking their truthfulness. These are only a few examples of Christians I've known who did not understand that "others" in the Golden Rule included the car dealer, one's spouse, and even politicians. Nor did they understand that "in everything" included car trades, marriage, and e-mails.

The Golden Rule is such a clear guideline for walking in the footsteps of Jesus, but none of us lives it perfectly all the time. When and with whom do you have trouble following the Golden Rule? This moment, as you are reading about the way of Jesus, is the perfect time to ask God's grace for times that you have forgotten the Golden Rule and to recommit yourself to living it—in everything.

Lord, forgive me for the times and places when I did not do to others what I would want them to do to me. Holy Spirit, prompt my conscience so that I might see the blind spots I have, and might, in everything, treat others the way I would want to be treated. Amen.

Saturday

"Listen! A sower went out to sow. And as he sowed, some seeds fell on the path, and the birds came and ate them up. Other seeds fell on rocky ground, where they did not have much soil, and they sprang up quickly, since they had no depth of soil. But when the sun rose, they were scorched; and since they had no root, they withered away. Other seeds fell among thorns, and the thorns grew up and choked them. Other seeds fell on good soil and brought forth grain, some a hundredfold, some sixty, some thirty. Let anyone with ears listen!" (Matthew 13:3-9 NRSV)

PARABLES ARE SIMPLE STORIES or metaphors in which some dimension of faith is explained by drawing upon analogies from everyday life. Jesus often spoke in parables and frequently used agricultural metaphors or stories.

In the Parable of the Sower, Jesus described four ways

that people respond to the preaching and teaching of God's kingdom. The seed in the parable is the message of the Kingdom. The sower is Jesus and all who come after him in teaching, preaching, or sharing the message. The four soil types represent different ways that people respond to the message—that is, different conditions of the heart and, consequently, the impact of the Kingdom on the lives of various hearers and ultimately on the world.

The parable is an invitation to spiritual self-examination. We're meant to ask what type of soil we represent and to consider the "fruit" we bear in our lives. Is your soul like the hard path where the message of the Kingdom never really sinks in and takes hold? Is your soul like the rocky ground where the message of the Kingdom begins to take hold but the roots never go deep? When adversity strikes, do you quickly fall away from

God's path? Perhaps your soul is like soil covered with thistles, so that the cares of the world and the desire for wealth choke out your quest for God's kingdom. The hope, of course, is that your heart is like the deep, rich soil that produces a harvest 30, 60, or 100 times over.

What does this last kind of heart look like? To me, it looks like Linda. Linda went to church her whole life, but she told me that for years her faith remained at a fairly superficial level. In her twenties, as a young mother, Linda cultivated a deeper relationship with Christ than she had known before. The message of the Kingdom really began to take root in her life.

Serving others became an increasingly important part of Linda's life. Most recently she has been volunteering eight to ten hours a week to coordinate our church's work with six urban core schools, most of whose students come from families living in poverty. She oversees ministries that deploy over 1,000 people from our church in everything from painting, to tutoring, to serving as pen pals, and to running book fairs. The work she makes possible has touched over 1,200 children and their families and may give them a fighting chance of rising out of poverty. The message of the Kingdom took root in her life, and it produced a 1,200-fold harvest.

Most of us will not see a harvest so dramatic, but we are each meant to bear fruit by living our faith so that others experience the reign of God. What kind of soil are you?

Lord, I want my heart to be like the rich, deep soil in the parable. I want my faith to grow deep and in turn to lead me to a life of love in action. Help me to do this, I pray. Amen.

Week Four

CALMING THE STORM
The Sea of Galilee

On that day, when evening had come, he said to them, "Let us go across to the other side." And leaving the crowd behind, they took him with them in the boat, just as he was. Other boats were with him. A great windstorm arose, and the waves beat into the boat, so that the boat was already being swamped. But he was in the stern, asleep on the cushion; and they woke him up and said to him, "Teacher, do you not care that we are perishing?" He woke up and rebuked the wind, and said to the sea, "Peace! Be still!" Then the wind ceased, and there was a dead calm. He said to them, "Why are you afraid? Have you still no faith?" And they were filled with great awe and said to one another, "Who then is this, that even the wind and the sea obey him?" (Mark 4:35-41 NRSV)

Monday

FISHING FOR PEOPLE

As Jesus passed along the Sea of Galilee, he saw Simon and his brother Andrew casting a net into the sea—for they were fishermen. And Jesus said to them, "Follow me and I will make you fish for people." And immediately they left their nets and followed him. As he went a little farther, he saw James son of Zebedee and his brother John, who were in their boat mending the nets. Immediately he called them; and they left their father Zebedee in the boat with the hired men, and followed him. (Mark 1:16-20 NRSV)

I RECENTLY SPENT TIME WITH YAERI, a Jewish fisherman who makes his living on the Sea of Galilee. I wondered what I might learn from this fisherman about the kind of people Jesus chose as his companions.

Yaeri was salt of the earth. I asked him what he loved about his work as a fisherman on the Sea of Galilee. He told me he loved the sea: "Every day is different. It is beautiful." Indeed, anyone who has been to the Sea of Galilee can testify to its beauty, as well as to how different it looks at various times of day and during changes in weather patterns. Those who have been to the Holy Land nearly always report that one of their favorite experiences was taking a boat across the Sea of Galilee, and most tours arrange for this.

I asked Yaeri, "Why do you think Jesus chose fishermen on this lake to be his first disciples?" His answer: "Fisherman make good friends. They are trustworthy and hard working."

Acts 4:13 notes of Simon Peter and John that "they were uneducated and ordinary men." The word *ordinary* here is the Greek word *idiotai*—a word that, at the time, signified untrained, unpolished in speech, or unskilled.

Jesus' first disciples were not the valedictorians of their seminary class. They were not those voted "most likely to succeed" in their high school class. They were men who likely did not finish school. They probably wouldn't have been anyone's first choice to lead a movement that would change the world.

When I think of them, I am reminded of a retired pastor I know. He struggled with stuttering his entire life. He was teased and harassed as a boy. But as a young man he heard God calling him to fish for people by becoming a preacher. This seemed to be an impossible calling; nevertheless he said, "Here I am, Lord." He went to school and ultimately became a Pentecostal preacher. He continued to stutter his entire life, but an interesting thing happened to him when he would stand in the pulpit to preach: his stuttering went away, and instead he delivered, with power and eloquence, the message of Christ.

Ultimately God used him to build a church with many thousands of people in a low-income community. The church included former prostitutes and drug dealers worshiping side-by-side with business leaders and educators. It was one of the city's most diverse and dynamic congregations.

God seems to delight in using the *idiotai*—the ordinary, common, nothing-special kind of folks. Paul writes, "God chose what is foolish in the world to shame the wise… so that no one might boast in the presence of God" (1 Corinthians 1:27, 29). Jesus comes to all of us who claim to be his disciples, calling us to follow him and he'll make us fishers of people. Are you willing to say yes?

Lord, help me to follow you faithfully, to be willing to lay down my net and join in your mission of fishing for people. Amen.

Tuesday

An Inconvenient Faith

Once while Jesus was standing beside the lake of Gennesaret, and the crowd was pressing in on him to hear the word of God, he saw two boats there at the shore of the lake; the fishermen had gone out of them and were washing their nets. He got into one of the boats, the one belonging to Simon, and asked him to put out a little way from the shore. Then he sat down and taught the crowds from the boat. When he had finished speaking, he said to Simon, "Put out into the deep water and let down your nets for a catch." Simon answered, "Master, we have worked all night long but have caught nothing. Yet if you say so, I will let down the nets." When they had done this, they caught so many fish that their nets were beginning to break. (Luke 5:1-6 NRSV)

Simon had been out fishing all night. Coming back to clean his nets, he was tired and ready to go home and get some sleep. That's when Jesus interrupted him to ask a favor: "Simon, the people are pressing in. Can I bother you to take me a few feet off shore and let me teach from your boat?" (Luke 5:4). How do you think Simon felt? I imagine him feeling inconvenienced, a little put out by the request. Ultimately, though, he obliged.

When Jesus finished preaching from the boat, he turned to Simon and said, "Let's go fishing, Simon." Simon protested at first but finally relented, saying, "Yet if you say so…" (Luke 5:5). With that, in resignation and likely some irritation, Simon took the boat out from shore.

Jesus often asks us to do things that are inconvenient. Most of us, I suspect, would prefer a convenient faith. I want Jesus to work around my schedule and never to ask me to do anything too troubling. And by the way, if he wants to borrow a house, car, boat, or tools, I'd prefer that he borrow someone else's!

One of the ministries of our church distributes beds, blankets, and pajamas to low-income children who have no beds and sleep on the floor. We do this as a part of our partnership with six elementary schools in low-income neighborhoods of Kansas City. I love this ministry.

Recently, one of the leaders who organizes the ministry asked me if I would join her team in distributing beds on a Sunday afternoon. My typical routine on Sundays includes preaching three times Sunday morning, going home to eat lunch and take a nap, and then going back to preach one last time Sunday night. The volunteer was asking me to give up my rest time, drive thirty minutes each way to the school, and meet the recipients and her team members. I'll be honest: my initial reaction was to thank her but say that I couldn't do it. After all, I had a good excuse. She would understand. But something (Someone?) nudged me and my wife to join them.

So LaVon and I ate a quick bite and went down to Wheatley Elementary School to visit with recipients and servants, as our church gave away forty beds for children who had been sleeping on the floor. I arrived at the school exhausted, but I left energized. Watching the children with their new beds, praying with families, seeing the blessing that took place—all of it filled me with a sense of renewed passion and joy.

In the end, Simon agreed to be inconvenienced by Jesus. When, against his wishes, he let down his nets, they were filled to overflowing. Will you allow Jesus to inconvenience you?

Lord, help me to pay attention to your nudges and to say yes when you interrupt or ask something inconvenient of me. Amen.

Wednesday

GREAT-TASTING BAIT

Jesus said to Simon, "Do not be afraid; from now on you will be catching people." When they had brought their boats to shore, they left everything and followed him. (Luke 5:10b-11 NRSV)

JESUS CALLED THE FISHERMEN TO FOLLOW him and he would make them fishers of people. This is a powerful metaphor. We're all called to fish for people. In fact, this is the primary way by which people come to faith and are added to God's kingdom.

Last year I went on a fishing trip to Canada with a few friends in the church. I had never been on a fishing trip before. Each of us on the trip was partnered with a guide. We would float down the river in small boats. Suddenly our guide would say, "There! Trout love areas like that.

Hurry, cast right there." We would gently cast, leaving our fly on the surface of the water. Whoosh! A trout would rise and take the fly. "Set the hook!" our guide would shout. Then we would slowly reel in the fish, bring it out of the water in a net, hold it to admire its beauty, and release it back to the stream. The experience was absolutely exhilarating!

On that trip, I couldn't help but think about the parallels between fishing for trout and fishing for people. In both cases it's important to go where the fish are. One evening not long ago, I sat in a bar by myself having supper. LaVon was out of town. I was working on my sermon, and several people came up to talk to me—they had been to the church for Easter or Christmas services. That evening I fished for people. It reminded me of something I once saw in a coffee shop. A member of the clergy wearing a clerical collar sat drinking coffee and working, with a homemade sign next to him: *Open for conversation.*

In fishing for trout and fishing for people, the lure matters. For trout, your lure (a "fly") needs to look and act real in order to make the fish bite. For people, the aim is not simply to look and act real, but to *be* real—authentic, authentically nice, caring, and genuinely interested in others.

Finally, with both kinds of fishing you've got to pay attention. When the trout start rising, you'd better start casting. And when God brings people across your path who are spiritually hungry and open to being "caught," you'd better not miss the opportunity to have a conversation about faith.

Last week, I heard from a man whose wife had just left him. The man was nearly bankrupt and was so depressed he was suicidal. His friends said to him, "We think you need what we find every week at church. Would you come with us?" To their surprise, and I suspect to his, the man came. He wrote to me last week, saying, "My life has been changed by being a part of this church. Had my friends not invited me, I honestly don't think I would still be alive." I'm glad they were paying attention, that they were credible witnesses, and that they were willing to cast what became a lifeline of faith for their friend.

Jesus says to all of us, "Follow me, and I'll make you fish for people."

Lord, please help me to be a credible witness and to pay attention when you bring people across my path. Give me courage and boldness to strike up spiritual conversations with others, that I might "fish for people." Amen.

Thursday

One day he got into a boat with his disciples, and he said to them, "Let us go across to the other side of the lake." So they put out, and while they were sailing he fell asleep. A windstorm swept down on the lake, and the boat was filling with water, and they were in danger. They went to him and woke him up, shouting, "Master, Master, we are perishing!" And he woke up and rebuked the wind and the raging waves; they ceased, and there was a calm. He said to them, "Where is your faith?" They were afraid and amazed, and said to one another, "Who then is this, that he commands even the winds and the water, and they obey him?" (Luke 8:22-25)

HAVE YOU EVER FELT AS IF YOU were on a sinking ship in the middle of a storm? The winds howl. The waves crash over the bow of your ship. And you know you're going down.

I see a lot of people who are in the midst of storms, wondering if there's any hope. At times I remind them of this magnificent story from the Gospels.

As followers of Jesus we believe he is always in the boat with us. He promises to be with me wherever I go. But there are times when it feels as though Jesus is asleep in my boat. Illness, tragedy, adversity, disappointment—these are all a part of life. At such moments we cry out to him, "Master, Master, we are perishing!"

After Jesus awoke and calmed the winds and the waves, he scolded his disciples: "Where is your faith?" I don't think he was suggesting that the disciples could have calmed the winds and waves, if only they had faith. I think he was asking, "Why did you wake me up? Did you really think you would drown with me in the boat?"

Sometimes Jesus calms the winds and waves immediately. I've noticed that most often during my storms, the winds and waves take some time to die down. I call out to him, then realize he's in the boat with me. I remember to trust him and know that somehow he will see me through.

When my two daughters were small and there were storms at night, one or the other would inevitably awaken and come running down the hall to our bedroom, crying, "Daddy, Daddy, I'm scared of the storms!" We had a small couch in our room, and I would make a little bed for them. I'd sit on the floor next to them and say, "Daddy's right here. You don't have to be afraid." Soon they were fast asleep. I didn't stop the thunder and lightning, the wind or rains. Why, then, did my girls fall asleep with the storm raging? It's because they knew their daddy was close by.

During the storms in my life, I cry out to the Lord. I trust that he's in the boat with me and that he won't let me drown. I commit my life, my ways, and my problems to him; and I find in him my peace. Paul captures this feeling when he writes, from a prison cell, "Do not worry about anything, but in everything by prayer and supplication with thanksgiving let your requests be made known to God. And the peace of God, which surpasses all understanding, will guard your hearts and your minds in Christ Jesus" (Philippians 4:6-7 NRSV).

Faith is simple trust that our lives are in his hands, that he is always in our ship, and that he will never abandon us.

Lord, in the midst of the storms that inevitably come my way, help me to remember that you are always by my side. O Lord, calm the wind and the waves. Amen.

Friday

"IT IS I; DO NOT BE AFRAID!"

Immediately he made the disciples get into the boat and go on ahead to the other side, while he dismissed the crowds…. When evening came… the boat, battered by the waves, was far from the land, for the wind was against them. And early in the morning he came walking toward [the disciples] on the sea. But when the disciples saw him walking on the sea, they were terrified, saying, "It is a ghost!" And they cried out in fear. But immediately Jesus spoke to them and said, "Take heart, it is I; do not be afraid." (Matthew 14:22-27 NRSV)

ONCE AGAIN WE FIND THE DISCIPLES in a boat in the midst of a storm. These storms come up with some regularity on the Sea of Galilee, as they do in life. Only this time, Jesus was not in the boat with his disciples. Staying behind on the land to pray, he sent his disciples ahead to the other side of the lake. Once again it was dark, and the disciples were in the middle of the lake with the wind and waves buffeting their small boat.

This is the well-known story of Jesus walking on the water. Early in the morning, from some distance away, he saw that his friends were struggling, and he went to them to make sure they were okay. Like the disciples, we have times when the wind and waves buffet us, but Christ sees us in our moment of need and comes to us.

But there is more to the story. After Jesus walked on the water, the disciples looked at each other and asked the question, "Who is this man?" Matthew, whose version of the story is printed above, frequently describes Jesus as one like, but greater than, Moses. After all, Moses led the children of Israel through the Red Sea, walking through the water as though it were dry land. But Jesus walked *on* the water.

But Matthew is also clear that Jesus is "Immanuel," God with us. Matthew's telling of this story, whether he intended it or not, likely conjured up Scriptures in the minds of his readers: Job 9:8 (NRSV), which describes God himself as one who "trampled the waves of the Sea"; Psalm 77:19 (NRSV), which notes, "Your way was through the sea, your path, through the mighty waters; yet your footprints were unseen"; Isaiah 43:16 (NRSV), which states that God "makes a way in the sea, a path in the mighty waters."

Who is this man who walked on the water? He is one greater than Moses. In fact, he is none other than "God with us" in the midst of our fears, our storms, and our darkest nights.

I remind our congregation that the part of our church building where the congregation sits is called the "nave," from the Latin *navis*, which means ship. The church has long understood itself to be a ship, an ark in which salvation is found. I love the idea that when we gather for worship we are in God's ship. There, Jesus comes to meet us, climbs into our boat, and tells us, "Take heart, it is I; do not be afraid."

The phrase "Do not be afraid" appears sixty-seven times in the Bible, most often either on the lips of God to his people or on the lips of God's leaders, reminding people that God is with them and they don't need to be afraid. Jesus shouted to his disciples, in the midst of the howling winds and waves, "It is I! Do not be afraid!"

Whether the Lord was asleep in the boat or walking across the water, the disciples did not need to be afraid, for he would watch over them, sail with them in the storms, and somehow find a way to deliver them. He will deliver you, too.

Lord, thank you for coming to your disciples on the sea, trampling the waves. Help me to trust that you are with me and that I don't need to be afraid. Calm my anxious heart. Amen.

Saturday

> *Peter answered him, "Lord, if it is you, command me to come to you on the water." He said, "Come." So Peter got out of the boat, started walking on the water, and came toward Jesus. But when he noticed the strong wind, he became frightened, and beginning to sink, he cried out, "Lord, save me!" Jesus immediately reached out his hand and caught him, saying to him, "You of little faith, why did you doubt?" When they got into the boat, the wind ceased. And those in the boat worshiped him, saying, "Truly you are the Son of God." (Matthew 14:28-33 NRSV)*

HE IS EIGHTY-THREE YEARS OLD, this man I care about a great deal. He was diagnosed with cancer six months ago. The oncologist gave him little hope. His mind is sharp and his heart is strong. He lives on his own and still makes six-hour car trips to visit his children and grandchildren. He makes it to the soccer, volleyball, and basketball games of his four grand nieces and nephews. He loves life. But he lives with this news that he has cancer that can't be treated.

We prayed together last night. As we finished, he looked at me with tears in his eyes and said, "I wake up each day determined to fight this. It is hard, but I try not to think about the cancer. I keep looking to the Lord, trusting him."

Peter's attempt to walk on the water with Jesus is a favorite story of so many people who read Matthew's gospel. Peter, as he often did, showed a remarkable burst of initial faith and courage: "Jesus, if it really is you, command me to come to you on the water" (Matthew 14:28 NRSV). But as soon as the strong winds came, he took his eyes off of Jesus, became frightened, and started to sink. He cried out, "Lord, save me!" Jesus reached out his hand, caught Peter, and helped him into the boat. Then Jesus climbed into the boat with him.

For nearly 2,000 years, Christians have seen in this story the call to keep our eyes fixed on Jesus when passing through storms at sea. If we trust him and focus on him rather than on the waves, we find the ability to walk "even through the valley of the shadow of death" (Psalm 23:4 NIV). That's what my dear friend taught me once more last night, as he held my hand and told me his strategy for living with terminal cancer.

When you find yourself walking in the darkness through the wind and waves, what's your strategy?

Jesus, help me when I wake each day to place my hand in your hand and keep my eyes focused, not on my circumstances, but on you. Amen.

Week Five

SINNERS, OUTCASTS, AND THE POOR

Samaria

He [Jesus] left Judea and started back to Galilee. But he had to go through Samaria. So he came to a Samaritan city called Sychar, near the plot of ground that Jacob had given to his son Joseph. Jacob's well was there, and Jesus, tired out by his journey, was sitting by the well. It was about noon. A Samaritan woman came to draw water, and Jesus said to her, "Give me a drink." (His disciples had gone to the city to buy food.) The Samaritan woman said to him, "How is it that you, a Jew, ask a drink of me, a woman of Samaria?" (Jews do not share things in common with Samaritans.) Jesus answered her, "If you knew the gift of God, and who it is that is saying to you, 'Give me a drink,' you would have asked him, and he would have given you living water." (John 4:3-10 NRSV)

.

Monday

"The Spirit of the Lord is upon me, because he has anointed me to bring good news to the poor. He has sent me to proclaim release to the captives and recovery of sight to the blind, to let the oppressed go free, to proclaim the year of the Lord's favor." (Luke 4:18-19 NRSV)

JESUS' FIRST SERMON IN HIS hometown of Nazareth was very short—only eight words. After reading the text for the day, from Isaiah 61:1-2 (quoted in the passage above), he said, "Today, this scripture is fulfilled in your hearing." Isaiah's words defined Jesus' ministry. He was born a king, but he did not look, dress, or act like any other king the Jewish people of Palestine had ever known.

Jesus was conceived out of wedlock, born in a stable, and brought up as the son of a handyman in a town that was considered "the other side of the tracks." His father Joseph was in fact a carpenter, but in a day when homes were built of stone, a carpenter was in fact a handyman—building things, making tools and furniture, repairing farm implements. And with regard to his hometown of Nazareth, Nathaniel captured it well when, upon hearing where Jesus was from, he asked, "Can anything good come out of Nazareth?"

In his ministry, Jesus was most often drawn to the poor, the sick, and the sinners. He had special compassion for the nobodies, the ne'er-do-wells, and the socially unacceptable. It was this compassion that captivated my heart and led me, as a fourteen-year-old reading the Gospels for the first time, to want to be his follower.

This King had "friends in low places." He humbled the proud and lifted up the lowly. He reminded us that the truly great must play the part of the servant. He taught that when sitting as a guest at a party, we should take the least important seat. He demonstrated concern for the lost and great compassion for those who were considered lowly.

Those who follow Jesus find ways to show compassion, seeing others as Jesus sees them—as dearly loved children of God. In the process of building relationships, reaching out with compassion, and demonstrating love in tangible ways; we actually become more human, more the people God intended us to be.

I think about Gerry. An executive with a large telecom company, Gerry had an idea (the Bible might label it a "vision") of starting a Bible study for men in prison. God kept putting people and events in his path that pointed in that direction and reinforced his idea. So the following year he stepped out, worked with a nearby prison, and began befriending inmates and mentoring them. Today the program has grown to include more than two hundred church members who are engaged in building relationships and mentoring and discipling men at Lansing Prison and Leavenworth Penitentiary. Lives are being changed through this ministry—not just the lives of the inmates, but also the lives of our members who have been blessed by the relationships they've established with the prisoners.

Jesus befriended sinners and taught about a God of second chances. Have you made friends in low places? Are you learning from them and offering them hope?

Lord, help me to see others through the lens of your grace, and to always remember that you are the God of second chances. Amen.

Tuesday

FRIEND OF PROSTITUTES

One of the Pharisees asked Jesus to eat with him, and he went into the Pharisee's house and took his place at the table. And a woman in the city, who was a sinner, having learned that he was eating in the Pharisee's house, brought an alabaster jar of ointment. She stood behind him at his feet, weeping, and began to bathe his feet with her tears and to dry them with her hair. Then she continued kissing his feet and anointing them with the ointment. (Luke 7:36-38 NRSV)

I LOVE THIS STORY AND WHAT IT TEACHES us about Jesus and his way. It seems that he was eating in the home of a Pharisee named Simon, which tells us that he befriended Pharisees as well as ordinary sinners. As Jesus ate, a known prostitute from the town interrupted the meal and entered Simon's house. This in itself would have seemed scandalous to Simon. Remember, the word *pharisee* meant "separated"—Pharisees sought to distance themselves from sin. Yet a prostitute had entered his house! She carried an alabaster jar of ointment, which likely was the most precious thing she owned. Perhaps she had been saving this scented oil for the day she would be rescued from her life of prostitution by a man who would love her, not simply use her.

Had she heard Jesus preach earlier in the day? Had he healed her of some affliction or set her free from some oppressive force? Had he helped her experience hope and forgiveness and love? All we know is that Jesus' impact upon her must have been profound: she brought her most precious gift to give him, and wept at his feet.

We see in this supper scene two very different ways that religious leaders might view a prostitute. If you continue to read the story (verses 40-50) you'll find that

Simon was offended that Jesus allowed a prostitute to touch him. Jesus felt differently. He saw her anointing of him and the tears that went with it as gifts, expressions of the woman's gratitude for the grace he offered her. Jesus asked Simon a telling question: "Do you see this woman?" Simon saw what she did for a living; he did not see her as a human being, a beloved child of God.

A number of women who were drug addicts and prostitutes worship at the church I serve. Most are part of a ministry called Healing House, led by a remarkable woman named Bobbi-jo, herself a former addict and prostitute. Being around Bobbi-jo and the women of Healing House makes me more Christian. I have had the joy of baptizing some of them and their children. One of these young women came to me after church recently to tell me, with tears in her eyes, how grateful she was for the church and how God had worked through it to welcome her. Her sincerity and tears reminded me of what it means to be the church.

Simon saw in the woman with the ointment a prostitute who had no business interrupting his supper and touching a fellow rabbi. Jesus saw her as a human being, loved by God, and in need of grace. Are you more like Simon or Jesus?

Lord, it is so easy to judge others. Teach me to see people as you see them, and to love them as you loved them when you walked on this earth. Amen.

Wednesday

The Invalids

Great crowds came to him, bringing with them the lame, the maimed, the blind, the mute, and many others. They put them at his feet, and he cured them, so that the crowd was amazed when they saw the mute speaking, the maimed whole, the lame walking, and the blind seeing. And they praised the God of Israel. (Matthew 15:30-31 NRSV)

There are passages in the Bible that seem utterly out of character with God. One of them is Leviticus 21:17-23, in which God commands that no one who "has a blemish" or "who is blind or lame, or one who has a mutilated face or a limb too long, or one who has a broken foot or a broken hand, or a hunchback, or a dwarf, or a man with a blemish in his eyes or an itching disease or scabs or crushed testicles" shall come near the altar of the Tabernacle. (The Tabernacle, representing God's earthly tent or dwelling place, was the predecessor to the Temple.) To do so would be to "profane my sanctuaries." This passage prohibited anyone with a disability from serving as a priest, because it would in some way offend God. Such persons could eat the holy bread but were not to set foot near the altar.

Jesus, by contrast, offered a very different picture of God, and Christians believe that Jesus' picture is the clearest and truest image of God. This was in part the reason for his coming: he would be the "Word made flesh," God's Word incarnate. Jesus said, "When you've seen me you've seen the Father." Among those with whom Jesus spent his time with were the lame, the blemished, the blind—the very people Leviticus had excluded from approaching God's holy place.

Invalid was once a common term for people who had disabilities or persistent illness. They were "in-valid"—they didn't count. This is a term that seems to fit with the passage in Leviticus. But when we read the Gospels and see how much time Jesus spent ministering with "invalids," it seems clear that God does not see his children with disabilities as in-valid! He is constantly reaching out with compassion towards them.

This last week I stopped by a fall harvest party in the Student Center at the church I serve. The party was for our Matthew's Ministry—our ministry for children and adults with disabilities. The party was awesome. We have 140 children and adults with special needs, and I love them all. Some were dressed in costume. Buzz Lightyear was there, as were Zorro, a host of angels, and even Uncle Sam. When I walked in, I was greeted with hugs and calls for me to "guess who I am, Pastor Adam!" Fifty volunteers made the evening happen. It was a picture of the kingdom of God.

Our ministry to those with special needs started nineteen years ago with a little boy named Matthew. Today it includes one or two parties a month, a scout troop, a handbell choir, Bible studies, mission service, a bakery providing jobs for some of our adults with special needs, and more. Our Matthew's Ministry[3] participants come to the church weekly to help load 1,400 backpacks with nutritious snacks for children living in poverty to take home over the weekend so they have enough to eat. Hardly invalids!

Churches and Christians who are intentional about welcoming and including persons with special needs are walking in the way of Christ and continuing his work of saying, "You matter to God."

Lord, help me (and the church I'm part of) to see persons with disabilities the way you see them. Help us to discover the joy of welcoming all people into your church.

Thursday

Soon afterwards he went on through cities and villages, proclaiming and bringing the good news of the kingdom of God. The twelve were with him, as well as some women who had been cured of evil spirits and infirmities: Mary, called Magdalene, from whom seven demons had gone out, and Joanna, the wife of Herod's steward Chuza, and Susanna, and many others, who provided for them out of their resources. (Luke 8:1-3 NRSV)

W E TYPICALLY THINK OF JESUS traveling with his twelve disciples as he "went through the cities and villages proclaiming and bringing the good news of the kingdom of God" (Luke 8:1 NRSV), but Luke tells us that women traveled with him, too. So many of the Gospel stories involve Jesus' ministry with women. It is clear that he valued women, had compassion for them, saw them as beloved children of God, and, by his interest in them, demonstrated the value God places on women.

Jesus' attitudes toward women stood in contrast to the cultural and religious traditions of the period. Josephus, the first-century Jewish historian wrote: "The woman, says the Law, is in all things inferior to the man."[4] Women were treated as the property of their husbands and fathers. Yet Jesus treated women with value and respect.

Notice the kinds of women who were following Jesus. Luke tells us they had been cured of evil spirits and infirmities. What kind of infirmities had they suffered from? The Gospels report that these included internal bleeding, fevers, and maladies then thought to be caused by demons, though now these are often associated with mental illness. We also know that Jesus offered grace to prostitutes, women caught in the act of adultery, and a woman divorced five times and living with a man who was not her husband. We also know that Jesus was concerned not only for Jewish women, but also for Samaritan and Gentile women as well.

The women Luke describes were more than followers. They provided support for Jesus and the twelve out of their own means. We learn in the Gospels that it was the women who stood at the foot of the cross while the male disciples, with the exception of John, were in hiding. It was the women who went to the tomb while the men continued to hide. And it was to Mary Magdalene that Jesus first appeared after the Resurrection. She became the first person to proclaim the resurrection of Christ.

I don't know where I would be without the female disciples who have entered my life. My grandmother was the first to share Christ with me. My mom took me to church. Two women encouraged me to consider being a pastor. My wife has been my partner in ministry, and most of the best ideas I ever had were really hers. In the church I serve, half of our leaders—lay, staff, and clergy—are women. Our aim for equality is not an effort at political correctness but at congregational effectiveness. Women made possible the ministry of Jesus in the first century, and they make his ministry possible today.

Lord, thank you for those women who have come into my life. Thank you for demonstrating the value of women in your ministry and, through them, teaching us how you value women today. Amen.

Friday

On the way to Jerusalem Jesus was going through the region between Samaria and Galilee. As he entered a village, ten lepers approached him. Keeping their distance, they called out, saying, "Jesus, Master, have mercy on us!" When he saw them, he said to them, "Go and show yourselves to the priests." And as they went, they were made clean. Then one of them, when he saw that he was healed, turned back, praising God with a loud voice. He prostrated himself at Jesus' feet and thanked him. And he was a Samaritan. Then Jesus asked, "Were not ten made clean? But the other nine, where are they? Was none of them found to return and give praise to God except this foreigner?" Then he said to him, "Get up and go on your way; your faith has made you well." (Luke 17:11-19 NRSV)

In today's Scripture, Jesus was on his way to Jerusalem, where he knew that a cross awaited him. Yet, even as he drew near to his own suffering, he was mindful of the suffering of others. Perhaps it was this awareness that kept him from being overwhelmed by his approaching fate.

As Jesus entered a village, ten lepers approached him. The lepers were both Jew and Samaritan, bound together by their common affliction. Leprosy (which included a variety of skin disorders) was the most socially isolating disease of ancient times. Fear of contracting the disease kept people away from lepers.

Lepers were the untouchables of Jesus' day. The Law of Moses required them to keep their distance from others and to declare, "Unclean!" when others approached (Leviticus 13:45). Seeing the ten lepers and knowing the isolation they experienced, Jesus showed them mercy, telling them to go to the priests, as the Law of Moses commanded, and they would be made whole. (The story is reminiscent of the story about the healing of Naaman, in 2 Kings 5.)

To visit the priests, the lepers had to make a seven- or eight-day trek to Jerusalem. Just as they set out, the lepers discovered that they were healed. This, it seems, was because they had demonstrated a measure of trust in Jesus' words. However, only one of the ten returned to him to give thanks, and this was the primary point of the story. The leper was a Samaritan, an outsider, who came back to thank the Lord.

Expressing thanks is important, and yet often we fail to do it. Worship on Sundays is about pausing to count our blessings and give thanks to God. Daily prayer is an opportunity to pause and to give thanks. Cultivate the practice of giving thanks, and you will find a greater sense of well being in life. That's what researchers Michael McCullough and Robert Emmons learned in their well-known study on gratitude. They found that people who regularly give thanks are as much as 25 percent happier than people who do not.[5]

John gave thanks. He suffered from a blood disorder that meant having regular transfusions, as well as a host of unpleasant symptoms. Every time I saw him, however, he would tell me he was blessed and was grateful for every day of his life. John lived far longer than the doctors had expected, and I am convinced it was because he sincerely and persistently gave thanks.

Ten lepers were healed, but only one returned to give thanks. Which leper are you?

Lord, thank you for the blessings in my life. I specifically want to thank you today for…. (Name five things you are grateful for today.)

Saturday

Why He Came

He entered Jericho and was passing through it. A man was there named Zacchaeus; he was a chief tax collector and was rich. He was trying to see who Jesus was, but on account of the crowd he could not, because he was short in stature. So he ran ahead and climbed a sycamore tree to see him, because he was going to pass that way. When Jesus came to the place, he looked up and said to him, "Zacchaeus, hurry and come down; for I must stay at your house today." So he hurried down and was happy to welcome him. All who saw it began to grumble and said, "He has gone to be the guest of one who is a sinner." Zacchaeus stood there and said to the Lord, "Look, half of my possessions, Lord, I will give to the poor; and if I have defrauded anyone of anything, I will pay back four times as much." Then Jesus said to him, "Today salvation has come to this house, because he too is a son of Abraham. For the Son of Man came to seek out and to save the lost." (Luke 19:1-10 NRSV)

On his way to Jerusalem, where crucifixion awaited him, Jesus stopped in Jericho for a divine appointment. As he walked past a sycamore tree, he looked up and saw a man named Zacchaeus in the branches, where he had climbed to catch a glimpse of Jesus. Jesus called to Zacchaeus and asked to stay at his home. The request was shocking to the townspeople, for Zacchaeus was well known in the region, not merely as a tax collector but as the chief tax collector. He was wealthy, and his wealth had come by collecting more taxes than was due. Watching Jesus, the people grumbled and said, "He has gone to be the guest of a sinner" (Luke 19:7 NRSV).

But notice the response of Zacchaeus. Dumfounded by Jesus' request, he decided on the spot to give half his possessions to the poor and promised to return anything he had wrongfully taken from others. And note what Jesus said to the crowd that day: "The Son of Man came to seek out and to save the lost" (Luke 19:10 NRSV).

I have asked my congregation to memorize that verse. It captures the heart and ministry of Jesus the way few other words do. He said that the reason he came—his purpose—was to look for and offer deliverance to people who have strayed from God's path.

We in the church sometimes forget this. If the church is the body of Christ, as Paul taught, then its primary purpose must be to "seek out and to save the lost." Jesus didn't do that by preaching at Zacchaeus. He didn't share a gospel tract. Instead Jesus asked Zacchaeus if he could have supper at his house. He befriended Zacchaeus, in spite of knowing that the townsfolk would consider it a scandal.

How would your church do things differently if its primary mission was to "seek out and to save the lost?" Who are the people you are building friendships with who are non-Christian or nominally Christian? Is there anyone you believe God wishes you to invite for worship in the next few weeks?

Lord, help me find ways to befriend and share my faith with people like Zacchaeus, and to be used by you to help others see your light and love. Amen.

Week Six

Jerusalem

They brought the colt to Jesus and threw their cloaks on it; and he sat on it. Many people spread their cloaks on the road, and others spread leafy branches that they had cut in the fields. Then those who went ahead and those who followed were shouting, "Hosanna! Blessed is the one who comes in the name of the Lord! Blessed is the coming kingdom of our ancestor David! Hosanna in the highest heaven!" (Mark 11:7-10 NRSV)

Monday

WHICH KING WILL YOU CHOOSE?

The next day the great crowd that had come to the festival heard that Jesus was coming to Jerusalem. So they took branches of palm trees and went out to meet him, shouting, "Hosanna! Blessed is the one who comes in the name of the Lord—the King of Israel!" Jesus found a young donkey and sat on it; as it is written: "Do not be afraid, daughter of Zion. Look, your king is coming, sitting on a donkey's colt!" (John 12:12-15 NRSV)

LAST ELECTION SEASON, I RECEIVED three political phone calls in thirty minutes, hoping to persuade me to vote this way or that. Signs were in the yards of my neighbors. The airwaves were filled with commercials for each of the candidates. The presidential candidates and their supporters spent *over two billion dollars* trying to get elected. In the end, each voter had to make a choice as to which candidate should be leading our country going forward.

On the first Palm Sunday, those in Jerusalem were offered a choice as well. Three "candidates" marched into Jerusalem that week, perhaps on the same day: There was Pilate, accompanied by centurions riding on their magnificent steeds, planning to keep the peace by intimidation, preparing to crucify a handful of Jews who dared rebel against Rome's authority. There was Herod Antipas, ruler of the Galilee, who had taken his brother's wife as his own—an incident that shortly thereafter led to Herod's beheading of John the Baptist for speaking against that act.

There was also a third candidate. He entered Jerusalem not on a stallion, but a donkey. He came not adorned in gold and silver and silks, but in the clothes of a carpenter. His followers were a ragtag band of misfits, tax collectors, prostitutes, common folk, and children who hailed him as a king on that Sunday as he entered Jerusalem. He spoke of loving your enemies, praying for those who persecute you, and turning the other cheek when mistreated.

Which person would you have chosen among these three? The powerful and the wealthy who ruled by might? Or the peasant king who called his followers to conquer by the power of sacrificial love? As I awaken each morning, I always take a moment in prayer to hail Jesus once again as my Savior and King.

Lord, help me to choose you each day and to follow in the path you've laid out for me. You are my King and my Lord. Teach me to demonstrate kindness in the face of unkindness and to overcome evil by the power of love. Amen.

Tuesday

WHO DO YOU BELONG TO?

So they watched him and sent spies who pretended to be honest, in order to trap him by what he said….So they asked him, "Teacher, we know that you are right in what you say and teach, and you show deference to no one, but teach the way of God in accordance with truth. Is it lawful for us to pay taxes to the emperor, or not?" But he perceived their craftiness and said to them, "Show me a denarius. Whose head and whose title does it bear?" They said, "The emperor's." He said to them, "Then give to the emperor the things that are the emperor's, and to God the things that are God's." (Luke 20:20-25 NRSV)

SHORTLY AFTER ENTERING JERUSALEM, Jesus went to the Temple and found that the merchants and moneychangers had been filling their own pockets by forcing worshipers to exchange coins or purchase animals for sacrifice at prices well above market. Jesus drove them out, enraging both the merchants and the religious authorities, who also made money off the arrangement.

After that, Jesus taught in the Temple courts each day, and hundreds came to hear him. But the religious leaders were determined to trap him in his words, by leading him either to say something they could claim was blasphemous, or to say something against Rome that would allow them to turn Jesus over to Pilate as a revolutionary. In today's Scripture, the trap they set was a clever one. If Jesus suggested it was lawful to pay taxes, then he would alienate those who resented the annual tribute owed to the emperor. If he said people should not pay taxes, then he would be turned over to the Romans as a dissident.

In response to their query, Jesus asked for a denarius, the common coin of his day. The coin represented a day's wages for a common laborer and the annual tribute due the Emperor from every adult male in Palestine. Jesus asked whose image was on the coin. The Greek word for "image" is *eikon*—icon. This was also the word that was used in the Greek translation of Genesis 1:27, where God made human beings in his image—his icon.

The head on the coin was likely that of the reigning emperor, Tiberius, and the inscription probably read, *"Tiberius Caesar, son of the divine Augustus."* So the leaders replied, "The emperor's" (Luke 20:24). Then came the brilliant response by Jesus: "Give to the emperor the things that are the emperor's, and to God the things that are God's" (Luke 20:25).

Who could argue with his logic? The coin was struck in Caesar's image; render it unto Caesar. But you are another matter. Your heart, your mind, your soul were made in the image of God. Render unto God the things that are God's.

The Covenant Prayer of the early Methodists is an example of a prayer aimed at helping the one praying it to "give to God the things that are God's." I invite you to make this your prayer today:

I am no longer my own but thine. Put me to what you will. Rank me with whom you will. Put me to doing or put me to suffering. Let me be exalted by thee or brought low for thee. Let me be full or let me be empty. Let me have all things or let me have nothing. I freely and heartily yield all things to they pleasure and disposal. And now, most glorious and blessed God, thou art mine and I am thine. So be it. And the covenant that I have made on earth let it be ratified in heaven. Amen.

Wednesday

Then Jesus said to the crowds and to his disciples, "The scribes and the Pharisees sit on Moses' seat; therefore, do whatever they teach you and follow it; but do not do as they do, for they do not practice what they teach... They do all their deeds to be seen by others... [But] the greatest among you will be your servant. All who exalt themselves will be humbled, and all who humble themselves will be exalted. (Matthew 23:1-3, 5a, 11-12)

Each day during the final week of his life, Jesus was more blunt in his criticism of the religious leaders. His parables were just thinly veiled indictments of their hypocrisy. In Matthew 23, Jesus spoke in the Temple courts to a crowd of hundreds, perhaps thousands. He began with a warning to do as the scribes and Pharisees said, but not as they did. One has the impression that there were religious leaders standing in the crowd, wearing flowing robes and frowns.

Jesus eventually turned to speak directly to them: "Woe unto you, scribes, Pharisees, hypocrites!" His words may seem unduly harsh and designed to provoke, until we remember that he knew already that these leaders would put him to death. He saw these leaders as betraying the very God they claimed to serve.

What were the religious leaders doing wrong? They were filled with pride. They performed acts of piety in order to be noticed by others. They loved affirmation and being seen as important. They demanded that the people practice one thing, while they themselves privately lived by another standard. They developed binding rules that contradicted the spirit and intent of the Law they claimed to uphold. They tithed on every herb in their gardens, but failed to practice justice, mercy and faithfulness.

In the most graphic of images, Jesus noted that the religious leaders were like "whitewashed tombs"—beautiful outside but full of decay inside (Matthew 23:27). The leaders appeared righteous but were full of hypocrisy and wickedness. They were like blind guides. They strained gnats but swallowed camels. You get the idea. It wasn't a flattering picture.

Having said that, I now have a confession to make: I am a recovering Pharisee, and sometimes I "fall off the wagon." I find that nearly every part of Jesus' indictment of the Pharisees has, at one time or another, applied to me. How easy it is to pose as something you are not, to love being called "Pastor" or "Reverend," to stand in front of a congregation asking people to do something that you yourself are not doing.

The Greek word for *hypocrite* meant an actor on a stage. Are you play-acting your faith, or does it permeate your entire life? Are you like a whitewashed tomb filled with unclean things? Are your motives ever less than pure? Jesus indictment of the Pharisees is an invitation to self-examination and repentance.

Looking back at today's reading from Matthew, I am reminded of the call to practice what I preach, to live my life "for an audience of One," and to humble myself before God and others.

Lord, forgive me for those moments when I have become a Pharisee. Help me to live what I claim to believe. I long for my motives to be pure—please forgive me when they are not. And help me to humble myself before you, while seeking always to serve others. Amen.

Thursday

I give you a new commandment, that you love one another. Just as I have loved you, you also should love one another. By this everyone will know that you are my disciples, if you have love for one another." (John 13:34-35 NRSV)

Jesus...got up from the table, took off his outer robe, and tied a towel around himself. Then he poured water into a basin and began to wash the disciples' feet. (John 13:4-5 NRSV)

Then he took a loaf of bread, and when he had given thanks, he broke it and gave it to them, saying, "This is my body, which is given for you. Do this in remembrance of me." And he did the same with the cup after supper. (Luke 22:19-20 NRSV)

ON THURSDAY OF HOLY WEEK, Christians around the world gather to remember Jesus' Last Supper with his disciples. The day is called Maundy Thursday, or Holy Thursday. It is likely that *Maundy* comes from the Latin *mandatum*, which, as you might guess, can be translated as mandate or commandment. On this night, just before his arrest, Jesus would give his disciples three mandates: love one another, serve one another, and remember him in the breaking of the bread..

Love and serve one another: Sitting at the table, Jesus said to his gathered disciples, "I give you a new commandment. Just as I have loved you, you also should love one another." What does it mean to love as Jesus loved? While Jesus undoubtedly felt a brotherly love for his disciples, that was not the love he demanded of his disciples here. He demanded *agape*—not feelings, but selfless acts done to help, benefit, or care for another. Earlier in John 13 we read, "He now showed them the full extent of his love" (John 13:1*c* NIV). Then he proceeded to assume the role of the lowest household servant by washing his disciples' feet.

After washing their feet, Jesus said, "I have set you an example, that you should do as I have done to you." Loving by serving is meant to define the Christian life. Jesus said this would be a sign to the world that we are his followers. We live selflessly and sacrificially towards others. In this we become leaven and salt. We let our light shine so that, through us, the world glimpses God's Kingdom and what we were meant to be as human beings.

Sunday a physician told me how a man had come to her office the previous week. He said he was not a patient, but his friend was. His friend needed a $1,700 procedure that was not covered by insurance, and the man knew his friend could not afford it. The man said, "I'm here to pay for the procedure, but you cannot tell him who did this. Please simply say that the expenses have been covered." The physician told me, "In all my years of practice I've never had anyone do something like this." In this one act, the benefactor had demonstrated both what it means to love and what it means to serve.

The final command Jesus gave was to remember him through the breaking of the bread and the drinking of the cup. While we do this in Holy Communion, I've often felt Jesus intended something more. Every meal in every Jewish home included bread and wine. I wonder if he did not intend that every time his followers gave thanks at mealtime, they would remember him. This is what we do when we pause to say grace at meals. In this simple act, we remember him who gave his life for us.

Lord, help me to remember your love and sacrifice every day of my life. Give me the grace to love and serve others without a desire for recognition or repayment. Amen.

Friday

Then the soldiers led him into the courtyard of the palace (that is, the governor's headquarters); and they called together the whole cohort. And they clothed him in a purple cloak; and after twisting some thorns into a crown, they put it on him. And they began saluting him, "Hail, King of the Jews!" They struck his head with a reed, spat upon him, and knelt down in homage to him. After mocking him, they stripped him of the purple cloak and put his own clothes on him. Then they led him out to crucify him....It was nine o'clock in the morning when they crucified him.... Those who passed by derided him.... In the same way the chief priests, along with the scribes, were also mocking him.... Those who were crucified with him also taunted him. (Mark 15:16-20, 25, 29, 31, 32 NRSV)

Mark's account of the Crucifixion makes clear the inhumanity of those who surrounded Jesus on that first "Good" Friday. They were anything but good. An entire cohort of soldiers came together to humiliate Jesus, beating him, mocking him, spitting upon him. Jesus was crucified outside the city walls, and those who passed by hurled insults at him. (Crucifixions occurred on main roadways to act as a deterrent for others.) The religious leaders showed him no mercy, mocking him as he suffered. Mark tells us that Jesus was taunted even by those who were crucified alongside him. For all these people, it was not enough that they had successfully sentenced Jesus to die. They wanted to dehumanize him as well.

If we could step back and take a cosmic view of this scene, we would see God the Son beaten, abused, spat upon, crucified, then mocked and taunted as he hung dying. And his abusers? The Romans fancied themselves the champions of justice. The chief priests and experts in Scripture believed they were the champions of God's Law. The common Jews saw themselves as God's chosen people. The irony of the Crucifixion is overwhelming: God came to humanity, even to his own people, and they crucified him, seeking to crush his spirit as he suffered.

The Crucifixion is at one and the same time a mirror held up to humanity, making plain our inhumanity; and a self-portrait of the God who willingly suffered at our hands to redeem us, change us, and save us from ourselves. We are meant to see ourselves in the crowd at Calvary. Alexander Solzhenitsyn has rightly noted, "The line dividing good and evil cuts through the heart of every human being."[6] But we're also meant to see a God who suffers as a result of our sin, and who is willing to die in order to save us from ourselves.

Like the crowd at Calvary, we have the capacity and propensity to rationalize the hurtful things we say and do to one another. We are experts at justifying what cannot be justified. We, too, have turned from God's way in order to hold on to power, to pursue wealth, or to protect our wounded pride. We've made thousands of small turns away from God's path, and a few really big ones. Which is why, on Good Friday, we pause to remember that the Crucifixion was for us. We see the Lord hanging there. We hear him cry out, "Father, forgive them, for they don't know what they do." We see in the cross our need and God's gift. We kneel before our crucified Lord and pray:

Forgive me, Lord! Heal me, Lord! Help me, Lord, that I might, from this day on, follow in your way! Amen.

Saturday

WHAT IF JUDAS HAD WAITED?

When Judas, his betrayer, saw that Jesus was condemned, he repented and brought back the thirty pieces of silver to the chief priests and the elders. He said, "I have sinned by betraying innocent blood." But they said, "What is that to us? See to it yourself." Throwing down the pieces of silver in the temple, he departed; and he went and hanged himself. (Matthew 27:3-5 NRSV)

SEVERAL YEARS AGO I HAD THE chance to visit the place tradition says Judas hung himself. The field, known as Potter's Field or the Field of Blood, overlooks the Valley of Hinnom—Gehenna. Gehenna served as the city trash dump in the time of Christ and, owing to the constant fires that burned the rubbish there, came to be synonymous with hell. On the site of this field are the ruins of a twelfth-century Crusader church and a host of discarded tombs in the side of the rock outcropping. And there, in the middle of the field, is a lone tree, a reminder that when Judas came to this place, overwhelmed with guilt over having betrayed Christ, he hanged himself.

As I stood at the tree, a thought came to me: "What if Judas had waited three days?"

Many people, at some point, think of ending their lives. For most, the thought is momentary and fleeting. For others, who are overwhelmed by guilt, depression, or pain, the thought lingers. Tragically, a few will conclude that death offers the only way out.

Judas was one of these few. He had betrayed Christ. His friend would die for his betrayal. He felt there was no other way out. Yet I could not stop thinking, "If only he had waited three days." Had he waited, he would have seen Christ risen from the grave. He would have known that even his betrayal was not the final word. He could have fallen at Jesus' feet and cried out, "Lord, forgive me!" And what do you think Jesus would have said to Judas? Can there be any doubt that Jesus would have shown mercy to him?

Imagine what would have become of Judas had he waited. His witness might have been the most powerful of all the disciples'. Can you imagine him telling his story throughout the empire? "I betrayed the Lord for thirty pieces of silver. I watched him die on the cross. But on the third day, he rose. And he forgave even me! If he forgave me, what can he do for you?"

In our lives, we have moments that seem overwhelmingly bleak. We make a mess of things and see no way out. Judas felt that way. But the message of the cross and Resurrection is that God is the Lord of second chances. In even the most dire circumstances, there is always hope. After our most egregious sins, there is the offer of grace.

In the darkest of times, there is an Easter yet to come.

Listen carefully: there is always hope. God is able to take the pain and despair of the present and bring from it something remarkable. You can't imagine it now, but look for someone or something that can help you find hope: a pastor, a family member, a friend, a suicide hotline. Remember Judas's story. Think about what could have been, if only he had waited three days.

Lord, help me to trust you in my darkest hour. Help me to remember that you can take something as ugly as a cross and turn it into an instrument of salvation. Grant me courage to keep walking when I feel like giving up. Amen.

* * *

If you or someone you know is struggling with suicidal thoughts, contact a suicide hotline in your area and contact the pastor of your local church.

Week Seven

When it was evening on that day, the first day of the week, and the doors of the house where the disciples had met were locked for fear of the Jews, Jesus came and stood among them and said, "Peace be with you." After he said this, he showed them his hands and his side. Then the disciples rejoiced when they saw the Lord. Jesus said to them again, "Peace be with you. As the Father has sent me, so I send you." When he had said this, he breathed on them and said to them, "Receive the Holy Spirit. If you forgive the sins of any, they are forgiven them; if you retain the sins of any, they are retained." (John 20:19-23 NRSV)

Monday

THE GARDENER

But Mary stood weeping outside the tomb. . . . She turned around and saw Jesus standing there, but she did not know that it was Jesus. Jesus said to her, "Woman, why are you weeping? Whom are you looking for?" Supposing him to be the gardener, she said to him, "Sir, if you have carried him away, tell me where you have laid him, and I will take him away." Jesus said to her, "Mary!" She turned and said to him in Hebrew, "Rabbouni!" (which means Teacher). (John 20:11, 14-16)

JOHN'S EASTER STORY IS MOVING and profound. In his gospel, he intends to do more than tell us what happened. His stories and their details are meant to show us what the story means.

Mary stood weeping outside the tomb. The stone had been rolled away. Jesus' body was not there. She did not yet understand. To her grief had been added the painful thought that someone had taken Jesus' body from the tomb to further humiliate him.

Composer C. Austin Miles penned his well-loved hymn "In the Garden" after reading John's account of the Resurrection. It is sung in Mary's voice: "I come to the garden alone, while the dew is still on the roses." Suddenly Jesus appears next to Mary, but she doesn't recognize him. Since the tomb was located in a garden, Mary thought at first that Jesus was the gardener.

This mention of the garden, with Jesus seeming to be the gardener, only appears in John's gospel. John wants the reader to connect the dots between this garden and the Garden of Eden. Remember, John begins his gospel pointing back to the Garden of Eden by echoing the opening words of Genesis: "In the beginning…" (John 1:1). John wants us to see that what happened in Eden—

the loss of paradise—was being reversed in Jesus' death and resurrection. In Genesis, God had said, "In the day you eat of the forbidden fruit you will die." The archetypal story of Adam and Eve in that first garden point to the pain and death that come when we turn from God's way. But in this garden—where Jesus is crucified, is buried, and then emerges from the tomb—he takes away the sting of our sin, and he conquers human mortality.

When I wrote the companion book to this devotional, I described a woman named Joyce and her cancer diagnosis. In the month between the writing of that book and this one, Joyce died. A day or so before her passing, I stood by her bedside at the Hospice House. Her family was there. One of our worship leaders sang some of her favorite songs. Joyce faced her death with confidence and hope, and she instilled these in her husband, children, and grandchildren. She found hope in the story of

Christ's resurrection. And with C. Austin Miles she would sing, "And He walks with me, and He talks with me, / And He tells me I am His own; / And the joy we share as we tarry there, / None other has ever known."[7]

Lord, help me to trust in the hope of Easter—that you live and walk with me, and that you have conquered death. I believe that because you live, I shall live also. I entrust my life to you. Amen.

Tuesday

But Thomas (who was called the Twin), one of the twelve, was not with them when Jesus came. So the other disciples told him, "We have seen the Lord." But he said to them, "Unless I see the mark of the nails in his hands, and put my finger in the mark of the nails and my hand in his side, I will not believe." (John 20:24-25 NRSV)

MICHAEL WAS A GUIDE ON MY FIRST trip to Israel. He was Jewish, but it was obvious he knew more about Jesus than the average Christian. As Michael described the various places we went, he assumed more New Testament knowledge than some of our people had, and I would have to stop and explain what he had just said. Michael was more like a professor of New Testament than a Holy Land guide.

At one point, away from the rest of my group, I asked him, "Michael, you genuinely seem to love Jesus, yet you are not a Christian. Tell me about this." He said, "I do love him. I love what he taught. I love what he did. I love the way he cared for the sick and the broken. I grieve the tragedy of his death and believe he gave his life to demonstrate the path of love, and to show God's love." I said, "Michael, it sounds like you are a Christ-follower." He responded, "My only problem is that I can't find the faith to believe in the Resurrection."

Michael was not the first to struggle with the concept of Jesus' resurrection. In Luke's gospel, the women were the first to meet the risen Christ, but when they told the disciples that he was risen, "these words seemed to them an idle tale, and they did not believe them" (Luke 24:11 NRSV). When Jesus finally appeared to the disciples, Thomas was not with them, so he did not believe. In fact, *ten disciples* told him they had seen Christ risen, and still he refused to believe. His skepticism earned him the nickname "Doubting Thomas." Matthew, in his account, depicts the disciples seeing the resurrected Christ for the first time in Galilee when he gave the great commission. Matthew notes, "When they saw him, they worshiped him; but some doubted" (Matthew 28:17 NRSV).

I think Jesus had great empathy for doubters. He knew the Resurrection would be hard to believe, which is why, after appearing to Thomas he said, "Because you have seen me, you have believed; blessed are those who have not seen and yet believed" (John 20:29 NIV).

The first time I read Matthew and Mark's Gospels I was not yet a Christian. I, too, found the Resurrection difficult to believe. Finally, as I read Luke's account, it began to make sense. I asked myself, "What would be different if the Resurrection had not occurred?" Jesus would have died on the cross, just the same. But this death would be a defeat, not the prelude to a victory. Evil would have won. Hate, fear, and bigotry would have been the victors. The apostles would have returned to fishing. Paul would never have met the risen Christ. The Great Commission would never have been given. The great message of redemption, forgiveness, and hope would not be known throughout the world.

It finally hit me that the story *had* to end with the Resurrection if in fact it was God's story. Evil could not have the last word. Death could not have the final say. I came to trust that God, who called forth the universe through his creative power, also had the power to bring about Christ's resurrection from the grave. Realizing this, I came to trust that the tomb was empty and that the women, the disciples, and Paul had in fact seen the risen Christ.

God raised his son from the dead. I not only believe this, I'm counting on it. But I still have empathy for those, such as Michael, who struggle with doubt. I assured Michael that he was in good company—that the earliest disciples of Jesus struggled with the Resurrection, too. I invited him to keep following Jesus' way and to continue pondering the meaning of the Resurrection. I suggested that one day he, too, might come to see the logic, and power, of the Resurrection.

"Lord, I believe. Help thou my unbelief." Thank you for your patience with doubters such as Thomas. Help me to trust in the Easter story and to know that because you live, I will live also. Amen.

Wednesday

ON THE ROAD TO EMMAUS

Now on that same day two of them were going to a village called Emmaus, about seven miles from Jerusalem, and talking with each other about all these things that had happened. While they were talking and discussing, Jesus himself came near and went with them, but their eyes were kept from recognizing him. (Luke 24:13-16 NRSV)

IT WAS EASTER AFTERNOON. The disciples were still reeling, having learned that Jesus' tomb had apparently been desecrated and his body taken. There were women who had reported he had been raised from the dead, but as yet the disciples did not believe them. Two disciples, a man named Cleopas and another unnamed disciple, left Jerusalem for Emmaus, about a two-hour walk from the Holy City. William Barclay's translation of Luke 24:17*b* notes that "their faces were twisted with grief."[8] They were on a journey filled with sorrow.

We've all walked on the road to Emmaus. Our road may have led to the unemployment line or the hospital, to the courtroom or the cemetery. One way or another, we've all walked on a journey where our hopes and dreams have been crushed, and sorrow seems to be our only friend.

Jesus came as a stranger to Cleopas and his friend. He listened as they told him, not realizing who he was, about the events surrounding the Crucifixion. When he began to speak, he offered them a different perspective on the events that had occurred. Then that evening, as he gave thanks for their meal and broke the bread, they saw that this stranger was Jesus.

Today, Jesus routinely sends us to be his representatives, as strangers on someone else's road to Emmaus.

And sometimes he sends others to us on our own road to Emmaus. Whatever our role, the key is to pay attention.

A man I know was checking into a hotel when a woman entered the lobby, upset and clearly struggling. She needed a place to stay for the night but had no way of paying and could only promise that she was being wired money the next day. She ran out to her car to get proof for the manager that she would be able to repay him the next day. While she was gone, my friend paid for the woman's room and quickly scratched out a note to her: "I felt God wanted me to pay for your lodging tonight. I believe he wants you to know that he hasn't forgotten you." My friend became the woman's stranger on the road to Emmaus.

A woman I know stopped in a church restroom during worship, only to find another woman there in tears. The two of them had never met before, but the other woman's face was "twisted with grief." My friend could tell that the woman needed someone to care for her, and she paused to minister to the woman. This was the road to Emmaus, and she would be the presence of Christ for this sorrowful woman.

As a follower of Christ, you have the opportunity to represent him. Pay attention to the strangers you meet. It may be that the Lord wants to use you to offer comfort and hope to those in need as they travel along the road to Emmaus.

Lord, teach me to pay attention to the strangers around me. Use me to encourage, comfort, and care for the stranger in need. Amen.

Thursday

THE GREAT COMMISSION

Jesus came and said to them, "All authority in heaven and on earth has been given to me. Go therefore and make disciples of all nations, baptizing them in the name of the Father and of the Son and of the Holy Spirit, and teaching them to obey everything that I have commanded you. And remember, I am with you always, to the end of the age." (Matthew 28:18-20 NRSV)

ANGLICAN SCHOLAR, PASTOR, AND writer R.T. France, in his commentary on the Gospel of Matthew, notes that its final verses, often called the Great Commission, are the climax and fulfillment of the entire Gospel.[9]

At the beginning of the Gospel Jesus is referred to as "Immanuel," God with us; at the end of the Gospel Jesus promises to be with us always, to the end of the age. At Jesus' birth the wise men, Gentiles, come to pay homage;

after his resurrection Jesus sends his disciples into all the nations. During Jesus' temptation the devil offers him the kingdoms of the world—not just their wealth, but by implication their power; at the end he declares that all authority has been given to him on earth and in heaven (Matthew 28:18). At the beginning of his ministry he invites twelve disciples to follow him; now he sends them out to the whole world to invite others to follow him. Throughout the Gospel Jesus has taught his followers about the kingdom, particularly in the Sermon on the Mount; now they must teach others to obey everything he has told them.

Jesus' Great Commission calls all who follow Jesus to invite others to do the same. But if we are honest, most of us are a little nervous about talking to others about Jesus. We love the quote, often attributed to St. Francis of Assisi, that we should preach the gospel at all times and when necessary use words.[10] We're happy to show the gospel to others, but often we pray that we won't have to "use words."

Yet the Kingdom of God on earth only expands as people who are Christ followers—people like you and me—share their story with others.

I became a Christ follower at age fourteen because a man named Harold Thorson was going door-to-door inviting people to church. I became a Christ follower, because a girl named LaVon invited me to youth group and Sunday school. I became a Christ follower, because a pastor and a youth pastor told me what Jesus had taught his disciples and invited me to obey. All these people showed me the gospel, and they knew they also had to use words.

There are people in your life who are not yet Christ followers. Some would consider the Christian faith if you were to tell them what your faith in Jesus means to you.

Make a list of people God may be calling you to share your faith with. Pray for them. Invite them to worship with you. Over a cup of coffee, tell them the story of how you came to faith, or the difference Christ has made in your daily life.

Last week a woman came to me after worship, saying it was her first Sunday at our church. She had felt lost for some time. Some good friends had loved her, and listened to her, and gently shared with her the difference Christ had made in their lives. The friends had described how they had found him at our church. And they had encouraged her, not just once but multiple times, to visit the church.

The woman looked at me and said, "Today I feel that I've finally found what I've been looking for. I'm so grateful to my friends who encouraged me to visit the church!" Her friends were fulfilling the Great Commission, and in the process they were being used by God to change this woman's life.

Who are the people God wants you to reach out to in his name?

Lord, I wish to be your disciple. Help me to follow you faithfully. Use me, I pray, to share with my friend your story, and to invite and encourage him/her to join me as I follow you. Amen.

It's been a blessing to share these devotions with you. My prayer, as I have written this little book, is that it might bless you, and that you might grow as you seek to follow in the footsteps of him who is the Way, and the Truth, and the Life.

I would like to express thanks to those whose stories are told in these pages, for the way they inspire me as they follow Christ. I am also grateful to Wisam Salsaa, to whom I dedicate this book. Wisam is a remarkable guide, artisan, scholar, and Palestinian follower of Christ with whom I have walked in the footsteps of Jesus in the Holy Land. Thank you, Wisam!

Adam Hamilton

Notes

1. Composed by Eric M. Bazilian, "One of Us," Joan Osborne, *Relish*, Island/Mercury, 1995.
2. Charles Wesley, "O For a Thousand Tongues to Sing," *The United Methodist Hymnal* (Nashville: The United Methodist Publishing House, 1989), 57.
3. For more information about The United Methodist Church of the Resurrection's Matthew's Ministry, visit www.cor.org/ministries/care-and-support/special-needs-matthew-s/.
4. From Flavius Josephus, *Against Apion* (trans. H. St. J. Thackeray; Loeb Classical Library; Cambridge, Mass.: Harvard University Press), 2. 200–201.
5. See Robert A. Emmons' book, *Thanks! How the New Science of Gratitude Can Make You Happier* (Houghton Mifflin Company, 2007).

6. From Aleksandr I. Solzhenitsyn, *The Gulag Archipelago 1918–1956: An Experiment in Literary Investigation*, (trans. Thomas P. Whitney; New York: Harper and Row, 1973).

7. C. Austin Miles, "In the Garden," *The United Methodist Hymnal* (Nashville: The United Methodist Publishing House, 1989), 314.

8. From William Barclay, *The Gospel of Luke* (The Daily Study Bible; Philadelphia: Westminster, 1956); 307.

9. Discussed in R.T. France, *The Gospel of Matthew* (The New International Commentary on the New Testament; Grand Rapids: Eerdmans, 2007).

10. Although scholars disagree whether St. Francis actually said these words, the concept of living out the gospel in one's daily life was certainly central to his message.

CPSIA information can be obtained at www.ICGtesting.com
Printed in the USA
LVOW12n1334300114

371636LV00001B/1/P